D0891728

Wittgenstein and Knowledge

WITTGENSTEIN & KNOWLEDGE

THE IMPORTANCE OF ON CERTAINTY   *Thomas Morawetz*

THE UNIVERSITY OF MASSACHUSETTS PRESS   AMHERST, 1978

Copyright © 1978 by the University of Massachusetts Press
All rights reserved
Library of Congress Catalog Card Number 78–53178
ISBN 0–87023–250–9
Printed in the United States of America
Designed by Mary Mendell
Library of Congress Cataloging in Publication Data
appear on the last printed page of this book.
Quotations from Wittgenstein's *On Certainty* are
reprinted by permission of G. E. M. Anscombe and
Basil Blackwell, Publishers.

*To my mother and to the
memory of my father*

Acknowledgments

Several friends and colleagues read this essay in whole or in part, made useful suggestions, and gave encouragement and support. I am very grateful to Robert Ackermann, Stephen Holmes, Stephan Körner, Ruth Barcan Marcus, Nancy Maull, Frederick Oscanyan, Roy Schafer, Gary Squire, and Robert Paul Wolff. I have two special debts. Robert Fogelin has shaped my thinking about philosophical strategies since I first studied Wittgenstein with him ten years ago. He read an early draft of this essay with great care. Rosalind Simson, as a student tutee, gave me the benefit of her insights into every part of my argument.

I wish to thank G. E. M. Anscombe and Basil Blackwell, Publishers, for permission to quote from Wittgenstein's *On Certainty*.

Contents

Wittgenstein and Knowledge

Introduction

Epistemology is the study of knowing. The philosophy of language is the study, among other things, of the logic and use of propositions which have the form, "I know. . . ." This essay is, first of all, an investigation of knowing and of claiming to know, and of the relationship between them. It is at the same time a study of the related notions of doubting, being certain, justifying, and believing. I argue that by attending to this particular intersection of epistemology and the philosophy of language we clarify and resolve some long-standing epistemological problems. Among these are whether there is ungrounded as well as grounded knowledge, whether thought and language are constrained within conceptual frameworks, and whether skepticism is a satisfactory epistemological position.

A vehicle for this investigation is Ludwig Wittgenstein's *On Certainty,* a collection of notes and remarks on epistemological topics written in the year-and-a-half before his death. The notes, in the form of 676 brief passages, are first-draft material, elliptical and oblique. The editors, G. E. M. Anscombe and G. H. von Wright, numbered the passages but did not rearrange or otherwise edit them. As Anscombe and von Wright observe in their preface, the notes were inspired by G. E. Moore's essays, "A Proof of the External World" and "A Defense of Common Sense." Many of the passages are explicitly about Moore, and many of Wittgenstein's examples of putative knowledge claims are Moore's examples. At the same time, *On Certainty* contains many acute general observations about knowing and its relation to knowing-claims. A major purpose of this essay is to elicit, explain, and assess these observations.

In addition, I suggest that *On Certainty* can be used to study Wittgenstein's innovative and influential philosophical methods in microcosm. My early chapters attempt to set the stage for a discussion of knowing by looking at the general notion of a practice. In doing so, I try to unfold a strategy present in all of Wittgenstein's later writings. Thus, this essay is directed not only at the reader interested in a general discussion of knowing and at the reader concerned with determining Wittgenstein's theory of knowing but also at the reader who needs a general introduction to Wittgenstein's methods and means.

Chapter one introduces the notion of a practice, which is explained by reference to Wittgenstein's notion of a language-game. I discuss what it is to be engaged in a practice and to be regarded as a "practitioner" by looking at learning and at the acquisition of practices. I consider the relationship of what we think, believe, and question to what we have learned and to what we can do. My purpose in discussing practices is to anticipate Wittgenstein's notion that it is only as participants in practices that persons can be said to have knowledge or beliefs and to make knowledge-claims.

In chapter two I consider ways in which the concept of a practice leads one to revise and refine the notion of an empirical proposition and the notion of a logical claim. Furthermore, I discuss the metaphor of a game as a metaphor for practices. Can practices be said to have rules and to be made up of moves which are applications of the rules? In particular, do practices have rules which govern the meaningfulness of utterances and of thoughts? Chapters one and two are general methodological chapters in which I spell out strategies largely attributable to Wittgenstein.

Chapter three is about justification. The thesis is that to justify a claim is to give grounds: it makes sense for one speaker to ask for grounds and for another speaker to give them only insofar as they share a conception of the sorts of things that count as grounds for particular claims. To share a conception of grounds is, in turn, to share a practice. Thus, justification occurs as one kind of move within a practice. Chapter three also offers a critique of skepticism insofar as the skeptic can be analyzed as characteristically demanding justification outside the framework of a shared practice (outside a shared recognition of what can count as a ground and of what can count as a matter in need of grounding). This critique of skepticism can, as I try to show, be found in Wittgenstein. There is an alternative account of skepticism wherein Wittgenstein himself can be seen as a skeptic. On this account, the skeptic argues that justification of claims is unavailable outside the framework of a practice.

In the fourth chapter, which is the heart of the essay, I take up those special practices in which persons claim to know, practices that I call "knowing-games." Here I consider the relationship of knowing and claiming to know. This, in turn, sets a framework for discussing Moore, Wittgenstein's critique of Moore, and the criticisms of skepticism made by Moore and Wittgenstein.

The last three chapters examine more specialized topics. Chapter five is about the relationship between grounded and ungrounded knowledge. It raises the questions whether some beliefs or convictions are held fast (or held to be indubitable) in all contexts and whether such beliefs can properly be the objects of knowledge-claims. This is an indirect consideration of the philosophically important and troublesome question whether there is a priori knowledge. In *On Certainty* Wittgenstein asks whether there are cases of claiming to know in which it is logically impossible that one is mistaken. Chapter five is an attempt to use Wittgenstein's own examples to answer this question.

The so-called problem of conceptual frameworks is the subject of chapter six. The problem can be generated in the following way. If my understanding of another's actions, remarks, and thoughts depends on our having the same practices (being participants in the same practice), then I cannot understand other persons as having practices that I reject. But this flies in the face of experience. I understand others to have religious, moral, and scientific beliefs and procedures in which I do not participate and which I claim to have reasons for rejecting. Furthermore, on what grounds can I argue that a practice that I reject is justifiably rejected, that my rejection has grounds? In chapter six I offer an account of the understanding and evaluation of alien practice based on disparate remarks in *On Certainty*.

Finally chapter seven raises questions about the status of philosophical discourse and philosophical knowledge. Is doing philosophy itself a distinctive practice with its own procedures? In answering this, Wittgenstein is particularly unhelpful because his own procedures seem to be at odds with his announced views in *On Certainty* and elsewhere. Chapter seven offers an account of philosophy as a practice.

The core of this essay is the nature of knowing and its relation to knowledge-claims. The early chapters are about practices because knowledge-claims and knowledge-attributions can be made understandable as moves within practices. The later chapters are about the special problems of ungrounded knowledge, alien practices, and philosophical knowledge.

One

On Practices

According to Wittgenstein, using color-language, calculating, and doing history are three examples of language-games, systems of activity which involve language and which are carried on by persons. I shall speak of practices where Wittgenstein speaks of language-games. In the first part of this chapter I shall draw together Wittgenstein's disparate remarks in *On Certainty* about each of these examples in turn. I do so with the purpose of explaining what a practice is by showing some general features of practices. I shall then draw some general conclusions about the nature of belief and doubt .

Let us begin by considering some uncontroversial beliefs.

234. I believe that I have forebears and that every human being has them. I believe that there are various cities, and, quite generally, in the main facts of geography and history. I believe that the earth is a body on whose surface we move and that it no more suddenly disappears or the like than any other solid body: this table, this house, this tree, etc. If I wanted to doubt the existence of the earth long before my birth, I should have to doubt all sorts of things that stand fast for me.[1]

1. All numbered passages quoted in the text are from *On Certainty* (Oxford: Basil Blackwell, 1969) unless otherwise indicated. Excerpts from passages and paraphrases of passages are followed by passage numbers in parentheses. All passages used or mentioned are listed in the Table of References to *On Certainty*. Compare passage 234 to passages 144, 159, 288.

Wittgenstein, like Descartes, is concerned to draw attention to the numberless matters that persons unhesitatingly believe. Like Descartes, he asks what it would be like to doubt these things. Descartes argues that it is the job of the philosopher to exercise such doubt: one must at least try to doubt all that one claims to know if one is to put knowledge on a secure and certain footing.[2]

There is an obvious impediment to the Cartesian program, one which Descartes recognized. To say that I *must* doubt a particular matter presupposes that it is the sort of matter that I *can* doubt. Wittgenstein stresses the peculiar difficulty of doubting such beliefs as those enumerated in passage 234. The difficulty is peculiar because it is hardly a matter of mustering effort for the job. Rather, the job is queer: the matters we unhesitatingly believe are heterogeneous, and we *cannot* simply decide and choose to suspend belief. What, then, can we do to understand the origin and status of these beliefs?

LEARNING AND THE ACQUISITION OF PRACTICES

Wittgenstein's strategy is to *examine* the question whether such beliefs can be doubted, i.e., to ask how this question can be answered. It is at least clear that "my life consists in being content to accept many things" (passage 344) and that such acceptance is not always a matter of indolence.

235. ...that something stands fast for me is not grounded in my stupidity or credulity.

I am not indolent or complacent in thinking that there are five toes inside my right shoe, although I have not recently checked. A chemist weighing a specimen is not merely complacent in the conviction that he is not having the mere hallucination of a scale. Rather, his having certain convictions and his not having certain doubts seem necessary to enable him to go forward with the activity of investigating. Of course, being content is

2. "I have realized that if I wished to have any firm and constant knowledge in the sciences, I would have to undertake, once and for all, to set aside all the opinions which I had previously accepted among my beliefs and start again from the very beginning." First Meditation, p. 75. Descartes, *Meditations Concerning First Philosophy*, trans. Lawrence Lafleur (Indianapolis: Library of Liberal Arts, 1960).

sometimes a matter of complacency. We must determine when it is and when it is not.

We may sort out beliefs in this way by looking at their origins and their role in thinking. How do persons acquire such convictions and become "content"? Wittgenstein says in *Philosophical Investigations* that persons learn by becoming "masters" of "techniques." [3] To master a technique is not only to acquire a skill, like driving or swimming; it also refers to becoming able to understand history, to identify colors, to multiply, or to speak English. The notion of a technique is therefore as broad as, and in fact coincides with, the notion of a practice. In discussing the acquisition of techniques, Wittgenstein draws attention to the special role within practices of convictions (indubitable beliefs). He asks how it is that a child comes to identify colors, to do simple arithmetic, and to learn about the past as history. And he answers this, in part, by attending to the role of indubitable convictions. I shall look at his comments about each of these practices in turn.

Acquiring color-language   When can one say of a child that he has learned that some objects are red or that he knows which objects are red? Wittgenstein remarks that one cannot ask a child who is beginning to use "red" and "blue," "What is this color called?" Nor can such a child yet ask for the name of a color. Such a child lacks "the concept *is called*" and therefore cannot yet be said to know about an object that it is red.[4] The child who is just learning to *react* "doesn't so far know anything. Knowing only begins at a later level" (passage 538). Of course, a child may be taught ostensively to use "red." But responding, however regularly and reliably, with the correct word in the appropriate context is no more a *sufficient* criterion of knowing "what this color is called" in the child than it would be in a doll. Such a child is, one might say, on the threshold of knowing about colors and not yet a full participant in the practice of knowing-about-colors because there is much he cannot do—or rather, there are many things of such kind that we have no way of telling whether he can do them until he does them. Does he have the concept "is called"? Does he have the generic notion of color? That is, can he ask

3. Wittgenstein, *Philosophical Investigations* (PI) (New York: Macmillan, 1953), part 1, paragraph 150.
4. *On Certainty* (OC), passages 535, 536, 537, 547, 548.

about any object, "What color is that?" Until he does and can, he is not really *ignorant*. An adult may know or be ignorant about what shade of red magenta is. The child neither knows nor is ignorant. Compare:

541. "He only knows what this person is called—not yet what that person is called." That is something one cannot, strictly speaking, say of someone who simply has not yet got the concept of people's having names.

Note two parenthetical points: (1) What we may say *about* the child is partly determined by what we may say *to* the child. If the child does not yet have the concept of color, we cannot instruct him about unseen colors, or say encouragingly, "Come on, you know what this color is called." (2) The learning child may suddenly begin to behave in ways which suggest that he has the concept "is called" and the generic concept of color. Until he does, the question whether he *can* is moot and the claim that he has the "capacity" is otiose. By contrast, an animal's non-participation in color-talk is predictable and stable.

540. A dog might learn to run to N at the call "N," and to M at the call "M," —but would that mean that he knows what these people are called?

Learning and knowing   Once the child is a *full* initiate and participant in the practice of experiencing and talking about colors, what is it that he knows? What kind of knowledge is involved in having a "concept" or a "set of concepts"?

Wittgenstein seems to try to answer this by asking what knowledge I attribute to *myself* in virtue of using color-language, and by asking when it is appropriate to claim to have such knowledge.

546. I should say "I know what this colour is called" if e.g. what is in question is shades of colour whose name not everybody knows.

But he recognizes that this won't do as a general criterion, for I know what a shade is called *whether or not* everybody else knows this as well.

531. But now, isn't it correct to describe my present state as follows: I *know* what this colour is called in English? And if this is correct, why then should I not describe my state with the corresponding words, "I know etc."?

These and similar passages are needlessly confusing because they refer obliquely to the following separate distinctions: First, as we have already seen, knowing-in-general what colors various objects are is not just a matter of emitting appropriate color-words but of being able to do other things besides, like asking the names of unknown colors. Thus, it is important to distinguish being able to emit appropriate color-words from knowing what colors are called. The latter refers to a variegated repertoire of behavior and of imputed experiences.

A second point is that even when it is a correct description of a speaker that he knows what colors these objects are, it is odd to *say* so unless the context supplies a reason for saying so. The fact that the speaker knows a color that others don't know is one such reason; the fact that the speaker is a child who has just learned color-language is another. The utterance is otherwise not *only* inappropriate but *possibly* of indefinite meaning for the following reason. Unless the reason for my saying "I know . . ." is evident, it will not be clear what sort of evidence will count in support of my claim, what sort will count against, and what will be irrelevant. Am I claiming facility in English, or that I am not color-blind, or . . . ? In such cases, insofar as my reason for claiming is unknown, *what* I have claimed is also unknown.[5] The distinction between knowing and being in a position to say "I know" will be explored in chapter four.

A third and different distinction exists between having knowledge in the sense of knowing facts and having knowledge in the sense of being master of a repertoire of behavior and the subject of a range of experiences. It is misleading to say of the child beginning to use color-language that he is gaining knowledge if knowledge is thought of, as it readily is, as a matter of knowing facts. The relevant distinction here is not the distinction between knowing how and knowing that but rather between knowing-how-and-that and simply knowing that. Knowing how to use color words *includes* knowing facts, e.g., that this ball is red, but it is different altogether from simply coming to know a set of facts about objects or a set of facts about English.[6]

5. It follows that one cannot completely separate questions about the so-called conversational implicature of a claim from questions about the meaning of the claim. When particular implicatures fail, the meaning is eroded. See H. P. Grice, "Logic and Conversation," reprinted in Donald Davidson and Gilbert Harman, eds., *The Logic of Grammar* (Encino: Dickenson Publishing Company, 1975).
6. Note also that when the child can be said to know that this ball is red, he cannot at the same time be said to know that this color is called "red" in English unless he at least can be said to have the concept of a language, a still more complicated matter.

The difference can be understood if we compare coming to know-how-and-that with the acquisition of a skill, with learning a game, or with learning to use a tool. Wittgenstein suggests these comparisons in *Philosophical Investigations*.[7] In each case, the learner is able to do certain things he was not able to do before. In the case of learning color-language, he becomes the subject of an organized realm of experience to which he did not have access, and his participation in this realm of experience yields facts about the world. The child who has learned to ask about colors has a tool for acquiring an unlimited set of new facts. He doesn't just have fact-knowledge; he has, in Wittgenstein's terms, "mastered a language-game."[8] I shall represent this by saying he has become a participant in a practice. The practice in this case is the activity, shared among persons, of having self-conscious experience of colors and speaking about them. A practice is like a game insofar as it seems to have rules; one who can use color-language violates the rules in calling a red object "blue."

The difference between having a practice and having factual knowledge can also be explained by the distinction between losing the ability to use a certain tool and questioning a fact. We say that one knows certain facts, has knowledge, when it makes sense to say that one can doubt, question, or test these facts. This presupposes that one has the "tools" to do so, that one has mastered the relevant techniques. An astronomer can check the distance of a galaxy; I can check the definition of "red." But what would it be like for the child who has come to use "blue" correctly to question and try to check whether the sky is really blue? To do so would be to lose a tool, to be impoverished in a way in which neither the questioning scientist nor astronomer is impoverished by questioning. The scientist who corrects a finding replaces one fact with another; the child loses an aspect of reality by losing something that he once knew how to do.

---

534. But is it wrong to say: "A child that has mastered a language-game must *know* certain things"?

If instead of that one said "must be *able to do* certain things," that would be a pleonasm, yet this is just what I want to counter the first sentence with. But: "a child acquires a knowledge of natural history." That presupposes that it can ask what such and such a plant is called.

7. See *PI*, part 1, paragraphs 67 and 83 (game), 11 and 14 (tools).
8. See, for example, *PI*, part 1, paragraph 71.

The notion that all fact-acquisition takes place through participation in practices is, I shall show, one of the most important points in Wittgenstein's work. It allows us to resolve philosophical problems about the relation of thought and action, the nature of doubt and certainty, and the justification of knowledge-claims. But before following up these matters, I shall resume explaining the notion of a practice by drawing upon other examples of practices than that of color-experience.

Learning to use names   We can compare initiation into color-language with initiation into the use of proper names, including one's own name. Wittgenstein remarks that a child can use names of persons long before he can say " 'I know this one's name; I don't know that one's yet' " (passage 543), long before he has "got the concept of people's having names" (passage 541). Only of someone who has the concept can one say, " 'He only knows what this person is called — not yet what that person is called' " (passage 541).

It may seem that learning to use names, as a practice, is different from learning to use color-language insofar as one's own name is idiosyncratic and specially familiar; one does not have a personal color-word as one has one's own name. This difference, however, masks a similarity between my certainty of my name and of what is red. What is red, like my own name, is something of which I am certain because of the special role it plays in acquiring and using a practice. Thus, Wittgenstein reminds us that we might not know our own names if they were used very rarely. We know our names so well because we use them so frequently (passage 568).

The point here is a general one about practices. As practitioners,[9] we cannot treat all relevant propositions as simultaneously dubitable. What does this mean in terms of our distinction between practitioners and knowers of facts? Descartes seems to invite knowers of facts to suspend certainty about each particular fact and reestablish it on a firm foundation. But, participating in a practice, one ordinarily cannot regard all facts as equally and simultaneously uncertain. The activity of doubting a color-fact or a name-fact ("His name is John") seems to presuppose that I have some color-facts or name-facts about which I am certain. My knowledge

9. I shall occasionally use the term "practitioner" as a specialized term meaning a participant in a practice.

of my own name is in ordinary circumstances such a paradigm. My refusal to doubt is usually not complacency.

The way in which some facts seem to be paradigmatic for a practice can be illustrated in color-language. I may be mistaken about "magenta" and may misdescribe a crimson object as magenta. It seems to me I cannot be mistaken in the same way about "red." This does not mean that I cannot be wrong, for I would be wrong if I had been taught aberrant usage. And it does not mean that I cannot be mistaken in special cases, for example, when I say that a white rug is red because it is under red light. But I cannot be mistaken about what color is called "red," as I can about what color is called "magenta." I have learned and used "magenta" in limited cases, which I may reasonably have misremembered. I have used "red" and confirmed my usage in innumerable cases; I cannot suppose that I misremember without impeaching my ability to remember in general.

This yields a very general point about the logical scope of doubt and possible mistake.

155. In certain circumstances, a man cannot make a *mistake*. ("Can" is here used logically, and the proposition does not mean that a man cannot say anything false in those circumstances.) . . .
156. In order to make a mistake, a man must already judge in conformity with mankind.

I can change my mind about what "magenta" is because my uses are limited and I can imagine how a mistake, even a systematic mistake, might have come about. The surface similarities between "red" and "magenta" cover this important difference: to think that I had been mistaken about "red" would, in ordinary circumstances, compel me to forego color-language altogether. This difference can be traced to the different roles of the terms in my cognitive history.

In just the same way, I ordinarily cannot doubt my own name. Wittgenstein remarks that if someone were to question his name, "I should straightaway make connections with innumerable things which make it certain" (passage 594). Thus, it is a fact about the language-game of using names that "everyone knows his name with the greatest certainty" (passage 579). Again we must distinguish the impossibility of making a mistake from the possibility of being wrong. "My name is T. M." *can* be wrong, and counterevidence can be found in exactly the same way as it can for any name ascription.

572. Don't I seem to know that I can't be wrong about such a thing as my own name?...

The point of this passage is that, as practitioners, we treat some propositions as paradigmatic for the practice. We cannot treat "This is red" as we treat "This is magenta" or "My name is. . ." as we treat "The name of the third man on the left is. . . ." We learn to name colors only by using color-words. Some color-words and names are tools for initiation into the practice and may take the character of paradigms. Wittgenstein, in one of the most important passages, says that "the *truth* of certain empirical propositions belongs to our frame of reference" (passage 83). There are special circumstances in which I will ask "*Is* this red?" but one thing I cannot mean by the question, if I am an ordinary speaker of English, is "Is the color I am seeing that which is ordinarily called 'red'?" Similarly, we need a special context for "Is this my name?" It cannot mean, for example, "Perhaps I've got the name wrong but the face is familiar."

I am not claiming that every practice involves paradigmatic convictions of the sort I have described. The notion of a practice is elastic, and I hesitate to make *any* claims about all practices. Also, I am not claiming that every fact acquired in initiation into a practice survives as a paradigm. We can surely imagine a child first learning to do historical narrative by way of the Greek myths and then jettisoning all such "facts" in a mature understanding of the past.

Learning to calculate: the possibility of mistake   Wittgenstein's remarks about learning arithmetic describe still another practice.

45. We got to know the *nature* of calculating by learning to calculate.
47. *This* is how one calculates. Calculating is *this*. What we learn at school, for example. Forget this transcendent certainty, which is connected with your concept of spirit.

The child who learns by rote the products of multiplicands does not yet know how to multiply. To acquire the technique of multiplying is not simply to learn a set of facts; it is to gain the capacity for generating an unlimited set of facts. One acquires the technique in part by learning basic, easy operations, which are the building blocks of more complex operations: "$2 \times 2 = 4$" has a natural priority over "$2 \times 2 = 44$," which "red" does not *inherently* have over "magenta."

In discussing the practice of calculating, Wittgenstein has occasion to describe the relation between the teacher of a practice and the learner. It follows from the distinction between learning a practice and acquiring facts that the teacher of a technique, whether it be using color-language or calculating, is not (and is not to be seen as) the custodian of special knowledge, of basic facts which are to be taken on authority. Wittgenstein reminds us that when someone is taught to calculate, he is not also taught "that he can rely on a calculation of his teacher" any more than he is taught "that he can trust his senses." In this way "explanations . . . come to an end" (passage 34).[10]

The point here is that the teacher imparts procedures which students come to employ autonomously. To say that we cannot check "$2 \times 2 = 4$" is not to say that we must accept it on authority. I have a procedure for checking whether 77 times 93 is 7161 because I know without resort to a procedure for checking that 2 times 2 is 4. Even if I count two objects twice over I will not really have "checked" the multiplication, and this is because I cannot have been in doubt, cannot have made a mistake.

77. Perhaps I shall do a multiplication twice to make sure, or perhaps get someone else to work it over. But shall I work it over again twenty times, or get twenty people to go over it? And is that some sort of negligence? Would the certainty really be greater for being checked twenty times?
217. If someone supposed that *all* our calculations were uncertain and that we could rely on none of them (justifying himself by saying that mistakes are always possible) perhaps we would say he was crazy. But can we say he is in error? Does he not just react differently? We rely on calculations, he doesn't; we are sure, he isn't.

10. It is possible to find counterexamples in which one accepts matters on authority which one could in principle work out for oneself. "Let's proceed with the proof from this point. I assure you I've worked out the prior steps and they're all right."

496. This is a similar case to that of showing that it has no meaning to say that a game has always been played wrong.[11]

There are two points here: first, in relatively complex calculations, there is a procedure for checking and a point at which the calculation is sufficiently checked; second, with regard to "2 × 2" there cannot be insufficient checking because there is no checking at all. The notion of a mistake cannot be detached from the notion of a procedure for checking. To insist that all calculations may be uncertain is not to appeal to a standard of certainty which is "outside" calculation. Such insistence is neither right nor wrong; it is simply rejection or abandonment of the practice of calculating.

One may, of course, recommend and use symbolic conventions such that "2 × 2 = 4" represents something false. This cannot show that ordinary ways of proceeding are wrong, but only that alternative ways of proceeding are imaginable. The possibility of imagining an alternative way arises only when I am comfortably familiar with my own way *as a system*, for the alternative is invented by varying my own.

We can now compare mathematical with empirical practices. Even in the most simple calculation we are possibly victims of oversight or illusion: whereas I cannot have miscalculated 2 times 2 and cannot in this sense be mistaken, I can for example have misread a figure. Our mathematical certainties are in this respect comparable to empirical certainties: we may distinguish ways of being wrong which infect mathematical certainties and empirical certainties equally and which (as we have seen) can infect paradigms as well as nonparadigms.

447. ...In so far as this proposition [12 × 12 = 144] rests on our not miscounting or miscalculating and on our senses not deceiving us as we calculate, both propositions, the arithmetical one and the physical one, are on the same level.

I want to say: the physical game is just as certain as the arithmetical. But this can be misunderstood. My remark is a logical and not a psychological one.[12]

11. See also passages 38, 46, 50, 212, 303, 304.
12. See also passages 448, 648, 651, 653, 658.

We can draw the following systematic conclusions from such observations.

1. The sources of mistake in carrying out mathematical procedures are the same as the sources of mistake in other procedures. Oversight and illusion are familiar and generally correctible sources of mistake. Reasonable men have familiar ways of preventing oversight and guarding against illusion. The possibility of making a mistake is understandable to the extent that it is also possible to do things correctly, just as having an illusion is understandable in comparison with seeing without illusion. "I can't be mistaken" indicates that I have checked my results sufficiently in those cases (like $77 \times 93 = 7161$) where checking is ordinarily appropriate and often needed, or that my claims are not of the sort which it makes sense to check ($2 \times 2 = 4$). What counts as sufficient checking will depend on the procedure, the problem, and the particular context. Sufficient checking cannot logically remove the possibility that I may be *wrong* (for example, in systematically misreading the numbers before me) or the possibility that I may be dreaming that I am calculating, etc. These remarks are equally applicable to mathematical and empirical procedures.

2. The incontestability of "The sky is blue" is no more in need of explanation than the incontestability of "$12 \times 12 = 144$," even though one is "empirical," the other not. Both are certain because they are elementary applications of practices, in the one case of the practice of using color-language and in the other of calculating.

3. To say that the propositions of many practices are vulnerable to the hypothesis of, for example, unaccountable delusion is not to deny that particular practices have their own special vulnerabilities. Thus, paradigmatic color-claims may be supposed wrong in the light of a hypothesis about eye defects, but this hypothesis does not infect name-claims. Similarly, mathematical claims are invulnerable to some hypotheses that infect other kinds of claims. The general difference between mathematical and empirical knowledge, and mathematical and empirical certainty, is explicable in terms of these observations. Wittgenstein says that mathematical propositions seem to have "the stamp of incontestability," that they are "immovable" as a "hinge" on which disputes turn (passage 655). And he says that this cannot be said about a proposition which expresses

my certainty about my name (passage 656). He makes the same distinction using a different metaphor when he calls the propositions of mathematics "fossilized" (passage 657).[13]

Wittgenstein's point is that when we suppose that mathematical propositions are incontestable or fossilized we say that no temporary cognitive defect, no supposed lapse of memory or visual hallucination can infect the understanding of certain mathematical propositions. I can offer a demonstration in the form of a definitive procedure to justify a simple arithmetic conclusion. There are no niches for doubts about my senses.

This shows not that mathematical propositions are incontestable but that they are not contestable on all the same grounds as so-called empirical propositions. This distinction is one thing we mean by distinguishing between empirical and nonempirical propositions. But empirical and nonempirical propositions are alike the sure foundations of practices, and they are equally vulnerable to the hypothesis of unaccountable delusion.[14] "We do not need to give way before any contrary evidence" in both cases *not* because we can simply *decide* to reject evidence that 2 times 2 is really 5, or that my name is really Jones but because the consequences in usual circumstances of conceding the possibility of error would be to impeach all putative evidence, to mistrust all propositions of this sort, and to abjure the practice.

Learning history   Thinking historically—thinking of oneself as a creature in the continuing history of the world, thinking of linear time and of past and future—is another learned practice, subject to its own hypotheses of logically possible wrongness. Might the earth not have existed a hundred years ago? The question here is not simply whether a particular physical body might have come into being at a time much later than we think but rather whether we might be *systematically* wrong in our thinking about the reality of the past. Wittgenstein connects this suggestion

13. See also passages 653, 654.
14. Compare Descartes, op. cit., First Meditation, p. 78: "And, furthermore, just as I sometimes judge that others are mistaken about those things which they think they know best, how can I be sure but that I am always mistaken when I add two and three or count the sides of a square, or when I judge of something even easier, if I can imagine anything easier than that?"

to the conditions for the possibility of learning the practice of doing history. He describes a student who interrupts his history lessons with questions about whether the earth existed at all a hundred years ago and about whether all of history is false. Is such a question legitimate, or is such doubt "hollow"? If such doubt is hollow, is belief in history hollow as well? Wittgenstein observes that the teacher will not regard such questions as legitimate, that the student might in the same way doubt the uniformity of nature, the justification of inductive arguments.

315. ... The teacher would feel that this was only holding them up, that this way the pupil would only get stuck and make no progress.—And he would be right. It would be as if someone were looking for some object in a room; he opens a drawer and doesn't see it there; then he closes it again, waits, and opens it once more to see if perhaps it isn't there now, and keeps on like that. He has not learned to look for things. And in the same way this pupil has not learned how to ask questions. He has not learned *the* game that we are trying to teach him.[15]

In summary, this is the application of Wittgenstein's general observations about practices and about learning to the practice of doing history. We can summarize the points.

1. The conviction that the earth's age is of a different order from the temporal relation of events on it and that all change occurs on the earth are initially not facts learned along with the other facts of history. Rather, treating the earth as subsisting through human history *seems* to be a condition of learning history.

2. It is misleading to say that the child believes that the earth existed a hundred years ago. He neither believes nor disbelieves; the question does not arise. That the earth existed appears as a *fact,* and as a questionable fact, only after he has mastered the technique of seeing facts as historical and seeing history as a practice.[16]

15. The example of the history lesson is in passages 310, 311, 312. See also passages 313, 314, 322; 143, 144, 147, 165, 182.
16. In chapter five I offer and discuss the following argument. If one is a participant in the practice of doing history and tells a science fiction tale (supporting a skeptical hypothesis) in which persons are wrong about the existence of the earth through human history, such a story will be intelligible insofar as it has certain indispensable features. It will involve beings which are historically linkable

3. We gather evidence for the facts of history, and our degree of certainty is determined by the evidence. But one's certainty of the not *systematically delusive* character of the evidence is not *grounded* and is not something one knows. There can be no evidence for this certainty since the hypothesis that one is wrong undercuts the very possibility of having evidence.

Even if we will not entertain the child's skeptical doubts, as in passage 315 (above), we will listen to the adult as skeptic, Wittgenstein suggests, insofar as he reminds us about the nature of our procedures and convictions:

185. It would strike me as ridiculous to want to doubt the existence of Napoleon; but if someone doubts the existence of the earth 150 years ago, perhaps I should be more willing to listen, for now he is doubting our whole system of evidence. It does not strike me as if this system were more certain than a certainty within it.

It is neither *more* certain nor *less* certain, for it is a certainty of a different kind. It is not the sort of thing which is grounded in evidence.

4. We do not *choose* our practices; therefore, we do not choose to believe in the past.

317. This doubt [that the earth really existed] isn't one of the doubts in our game. (But not as if we *chose* this game!)

We have no alternative to believing that the earth existed, just as we have no alternative to believing that $2 \times 2 = 4$. But it is wrong to think that we are compelled to do history or calculation; one can speak of being "compelled" to do things only where alternatives to that practice are possible and conceivable but placed out of reach. If doing history or calculation is a technique or an activity, the "alternative" is to be deficient in the technique.

5. The dawning of a child's first historical fact is not predicated on a

---

to the teller and hearer, beings which inhabit spatial and temporal loci understandable in relation to the teller's and hearer's locus, and so forth. Just as the practice of doing history seems to have its own rules, so too the practice of raising hypotheses about variant historical practices is parasitic upon the first practice and has *its* own rules.

prior assumption or belief about the existence of the world. (It is misleading to say, as Wittgenstein does [146], that in order to have "a picture of the earth as a ball . . . not altering essentially in a hundred years, . . . somewhere I must begin with an assumption or a decision.") Although the child trusts his teachers, his learning is not predicated on a *belief* about the trustworthiness of his teacher.

143. I am told, for example, that someone climbed this mountain many years ago. Do I always enquire into the reliability of the teller of this story, and whether the mountain did exist years ago? A child learns there are reliable and unreliable informants much later than it learns facts which are told it. . . .

A technique is not adopted on the basis of grounds; only in using a technique (working within a practice) does it make sense to say, for example, about the specific claims of a historian, that he has grounds.

On having procedures and practices I began this chapter with questions about doubt, certainty, and unquestioning belief. I have tried to explain Wittgenstein's notion of a practice by looking at particular practices (using color-language, doing calculations, using proper names, investigating history) because answers to these questions presuppose the notion of a practice. In each case, we have seen that doubting particular facts makes sense only within a practice—characteristically, when certain other matters are held as unquestioned paradigms. Thus, a certainty that is grounded on accumulated and persuasive evidence is very different from certainty about matters that seem to have no ground and need no ground.

In *On Certainty,* as in *Philosophical Investigations,* Wittgenstein warns that the grammatical form of different propositions may mislead persons into thinking that they are alike in use.[17] Compare "This building has existed for two hundred years" with "Historical time has existed

17. *PI,* part 1, paragraph 11:
   Think of the tools in a tool-box: there is a hammer, pliers, a saw, a screwdriver, a rule, a glue-pot, glue, nails and screws.—The functions of words are as diverse as the functions of these objects. (And in both cases there are similarities.)
   Of course, what confuses us is the uniform appearance of words when we hear them spoken or meet them in script and print. For their *application* is not presented to us so clearly.

for . . . years," "Washington's uniform was blue" with "Indigo is blue," and a complex multiplication with "2 × 2 = 4." Compare also "This is John's book" with "This is my hand." Now, let p stand for each proposition. In each pair, the latter proposition is of special concern because "I am certain that p" is not to be understood as "I have checked p sufficiently" or "I have satisfied myself that p" or "I rely on evidence that assures me that p." This is true in each case even though the examples, and the practices they represent, are in other respects very different. Wittgenstein is concerned primarily with examples of propositions that might misleadingly be assimilated to evidentiary conclusions, or conclusions reached by the application of procedures. (There is of course the tacit supposition that contexts are ordinary. In extraordinary contexts "This is my hand" may well have been said on the basis of evidence, for example if I were identifying my severed hand.)

The first proposition in each pair is such that ordinarily if I say "I am certain that p," or "I believe that p," or "I know that p," or if I claim that p is true, I do so on the basis of grounds. I can defend my claim by showing how I arrived at it. I can also anticipate the kinds of grounds on which I or others might doubt my claim. None of these things can be said about the second proposition in each pair. I can say of particular claims which I am able to support with grounds that they are true, but I cannot say this about the practice of history any more than I can say that history is true. We have seen that propositions that *look* like particular, and therefore disputable, historical claims are convictions that make possible the enterprise of history. By analogy, Wittgenstein questions the intelligibility of "I know that physics is true" (passage 602).

Within physics and history matters are proved, disproved, questioned, and known through the application of procedures for finding out, procedures that themselves change over time. Hypotheses are found to be true or not, but the enterprise itself is not said to be true or false. To ask whether *all* the propositions of history or physics or chemistry might be false or whether all my calculations might be false is to question the possibility of the enterprise. (And this is to be distinguished, although the distinction may be hard to draw and unclear at the edges, from questioning one *way* of going about the enterprise.) [18]

18. In chapter six, I discuss how we confront alternative practices in science, his-

169. One might think that there were propositions declaring that chemistry is *possible*. And these would be propositions of a natural science. For what should they be supported by, if not by experience?

That chemistry is possible is not the sort of thing that can be found out. Nothing turns on the hypothesis that chemistry might not be possible; one could never find chemistry, physics, or history *as a whole* to be recalcitrant any more than one could find all one's calculations to be wrong. Doubt and recalcitrance can occur only within a system of having expectations and seeking results.

247. What would it be like to doubt now whether I have two hands? Why can't I imagine it at all? What would I believe if I didn't believe that? So far I have no system at all within which this doubt might exist.

Propositions that cannot be doubted in any context at all can be distinguished from propositions (which are exemplified by what I have called "paradigms") that can only be doubted in very special (aberrant) contexts. Wittgenstein offers examples of both kinds without clearly marking the distinction. To apply the distinction, we must recognize both that there is *no* context in which one can say "I know physics (or history) is true," suggesting that this is something one might find out or something one might doubt and that there are only very special contexts in which one can say "I know that that is my hand" or "I know that $2 \times 2 = 4$." Such special contexts are identifiable case by case but probably not specifiable by way of general criteria.[19] Cases are those in which I identify a severed hand or in which I announce my newly acquired ability to multiply.

As a further complication, those matters which are dubitable (and subjects of knowledge-claims) only in special contexts are, tautologically, matters that I cannot *claim* to know without suggesting that the context is special in relevant ways. Nonetheless, it is a correct description of me

---

tory, etc. To say that I cannot imagine that physics is false, or make sense of this suggestion, is not to say that I cannot imagine that many of my generally applied procedures may be subject to unforeseeable revision and change. But such change is internal to the enterprise.

19. G. E. M. Anscombe makes this point in her paper, "On Brute Facts," *Analysis,* vol. 18 (1958), pp. 69–72; see point (4) in her summary.

in ordinary contexts that I am certain that this is my hand or that $2 \times 2 = 4$; I am certain in a different way than I am of matters I have found out. On the other hand, those matters which are not dubitable in any context will not bear this interpretation: I am not *certain* that physics is true (although I am certain that some paradigmatic facts of physics are true).

We can summarize much of this in the following three points.

1. We must look beyond the surface similarity of, for example, "$2 \times 2 = 4$" and a complex calculation or of "This is my hand" and "This is John's book." In each pair, the first is an elementary proposition that serves as a paradigm; it is the typical underpinning of a practice that there be some such paradigms. These propositions are pseudoempirical: they are not derived inductively or dubitable in ordinary circumstances. "If this is not my hand, so much the worse for empirical judgment" is not merely an expression of my psychological attitude but of the (logical) role of my conviction.[20]

2. From the difference between "This is my hand" and "This is John's book," we are not to conclude that the former stands in need of some ground but not an *empirical* ground. Rather the question of grounding doesn't arise because the possibility of doubt doesn't arise. To raise such doubts in the absence of specific counterexamples is to jettison the practice. Such doubts have the function of putting in question the practice as a whole; in principle, they cannot be assuaged by giving grounds. As Wittgenstein says, the process of giving grounds makes sense only within a practice. He asks, for example, what grounds one has for trusting textbooks of physics. To be sure, one knows something about such books, how they are produced, etc., but such evidence "does not go very far and is of a very scattered kind." Rather than having grounds for trusting such books, "I have no grounds for not trusting them" (passage 600). Moreover, "hasn't this trust also proved itself? So far as I can judge—yes" (passage 603).[21] Thus, whether we are concerned with propositions of physics, history, or naming, only some of our propositions can stand in need of grounds or stand vulnerable to doubt.

20. I shall discuss the distinction between logical and psychological points in chapter two.
21. See also passage 604.

249. One gives oneself a false picture of *doubt*.

331. If we ever do act with certainty on the strength of belief, should we wonder that there is much we cannot doubt?

To be sure, these remarks are all about practical doubt, doubt that affects practice and is reflected in what we do. This is the only kind of doubt with which Wittgenstein is concerned. In later chapters I shall discuss the relation of such doubt to philosophical (skeptical) doubt and to imagined doubt, doubts which are hypothetical.

3. Propositions like "This is my hand" are uttered meaningfully only in a special setting. Only then may hearers know what sorts of evidence may be said to count as relevant grounds for the utterance. I shall continue to be concerned with the special character of so-called paradigmatic propositions, which lie apart from avenues of investigation and which persons "learn" insofar as they become initiates into practices. These propositions have held particular fascination for philosophers. Skeptics, for example, have argued that if knowledge of such matters cannot be justified, speakers are not entitled to claim to know any matter which depends on or presupposes them.

ENGAGING IN PRACTICES: ACTING AND KNOWING

I have been speaking about the propositions, "This is my hand," "Physics is true," and "$2 \times 2 = 4$," and drawing conclusions about them as possible utterances. We have seen ways in which it is misleading to refer to them as objects of belief and as objects of knowledge. We have referred to them as ungrounded propositions and as propositions that need no justification.

Such a discussion threatens to distract us from the main point: the matters to which such propositions refer do not reach expression *as* propositions unless and until persons become self-conscious about their practices. In describing practices and practitioners, it is appropriate to think of such matters in terms of activity rather than in terms of cognition. To say that I cannot doubt p is not to speak of a cognitive disability. It is that my actions presuppose that I hold p fast and that they would otherwise be pointless.

Let me explain by citing some of Wittgenstein's illustrations. My determination that A believes p is often based on what A does (nonverbally) rather than on what A says. His actions create a presumption that his words often cannot override. On the basis of actions, I will attribute certainty, knowledge, doubts, or the failure to doubt.

7. My life shews [sic] that I know or am certain that there is a chair over there, or a door, and so on.—I tell a friend, e.g. "Take that chair over there," "Shut the door," etc. etc.

427. We need to shew [sic] that even if he never uses the words "I know...," his conduct exhibits the thing we are concerned with.[22]

What is the relation between behavior and the proposition that describes imputed belief in these situations? The point is not that behavior is evidence for the proposition, "A believes p...." Rather the imputed belief is a necessary part of such behavior: the behavior is understandable as the sort of behavior it is only in terms of the belief. To say that I may address you without believing that you can hear me, or that I may enter a familiar classroom without trusting that the floor will hold me up, is to say something incoherent. My behavior is what it is—a telling, a looking for—only if I can be said to have certain beliefs. (Throughout this section, I am using "belief" not in the sense of grounded belief or in the sense of surmise, but in Wittgenstein's sense of a conviction, perhaps never expressed or even thought, which is exhibited in behavior. It is misleading to confuse such beliefs with surmises, i.e., with groundable hypotheses.)

Suppose A behaves normally and disclaims belief. Wittgenstein describes someone who is supposed to meet a friend at the train, goes to the station at the right time, and says that he has no belief at all that the train will arrive (passage 339).[23] He acts normally, but claims to doubt. Consider three ways of understanding such expressions of doubt.

1. One may find aberrant behavior, in addition to the verbal claim to doubt, which fits the claim, for example, annoyance and irritability. In another case, A may tread lightly and claim to believe that the floor will not hold him up. Even in such cases, I will not concede that A *really*

22. See passages 428, 284, 285.
23. See also passage 338.

doubts *p* if I cannot supply putative reasons for doubt. Only in special contexts is doubting behavior understandable as doubting. Someone who claimed to doubt the existence of his hands, "kept looking at them from all sides," etc., might show the manifestations of doubt but "we should not be sure whether we ought to call that doubting. . . . His game would not be ours" (passage 255).[24] This is not to say that I can attribute doubt to A only in cases in which I too would doubt or on the basis of reasons which would make me doubt. But I have to understand his doubt as *grounded,* even if the same grounds would not lead me to doubt.

2. I may interpret the disclaimer as a way of saying that there exists a logical possibility of being wrong in thinking, for example, that the floor will support us or that one's toes have not been amputated. The following passage shows that this point is not a point about what is highly probable or improbable.

338. . . . [T]here *are* people who say that it is merely extremely probable that water over a fire will boil and not freeze, and that therefore strictly speaking what we consider impossible is only improbable. What difference does this make in their lives? Isn't it just that they talk rather more about certain things than the rest of us?

That which is probable is supported by a preponderance of evidence, and the claim, as interpreted, is not about evidence but logical possibility. A claim that *p* is probably the case implies that the evidence at hand will not quite support a claim to know. These suggestions mask the appropriate claim that evidence would not be sought or needed for these matters. Saying that such things are probable is misleading.

It is also misleading to say that such things "feel" sure, suggesting that it is a psychological matter and not a matter of the logic of practices that these things be certain.

524. Is it essential for our language-games . . . that no doubt appears at certain points, or is it enough if there is the feeling of being sure, admittedly with a slight breath of doubt? . . .
The accompanying feeling is of course a matter of indifference to us, and equally we have no need to bother about the words "I am sure that" either.—

24. See also passage 154.

What is important is whether they go with a difference in the *practice* of the language.

One might ask whether a person who spoke like this would always say "I am sure" on occasions where (for example) there is sureness in the reports we make.... If he does, our immediate inclination will be to check what he says. But if he proves to be perfectly reliable, one will say that his way of talking is merely a bit perverse, and does not affect the issue. One might for example suppose that he has read sceptical philosophy, become convinced that one can know nothing, and that is why he has adopted this way of speaking....

This second possibility is, therefore, the possibility of understanding "I doubt..." as an expression of general philosophical skepticism confusingly conflated with the language of practical doubt and practical certainty. In chapters two and four I shall discuss the implications of this argument for thought and practice.

3. I may, as a last resort, refuse to credit the expression of doubt and conclude that A's actions belie his words. I will either fail to understand why he says what he does or suspect him of deceit.

Basic knowledge or basic action?   So far I have looked at behavior as the manifestation of belief and doubt in other persons. Unless A behaves in certain ways and unless I can impute appropriate grounds to A, I cannot understand A's use of the word "doubt" as a claim to doubt *p*. But, equally important, unless I behave in certain ways (which go beyond saying "I doubt *p*" and involve having certain kinds of grounds), it is not possible for me to regard myself as doubting *p* in any sense of doubt which relates to practices. Doubting is not a matter of regarding an isolated proposition in a special way; if this hold for A's doubts, it holds for mine as well. As long as I continue to act in certain ways, I *am not* doubting certain things. Wittgenstein's example of the man at the railway station is no more intelligible if I imagine myself as that man.

In several important passages, Wittgenstein tries to make clear the relation between one's own actions and one's own thoughts about propositions which characterize such actions and their setting. He says that when "giving grounds... comes to an end,... the end is not certain propositions striking us immediately as true; i.e., it is not a kind of seeing on our part; it is our acting, which lies at the bottom of the language-game" (passage 204). Further, he remarks that "my life consists in my being content to accept many things" (passage 344).[25] It follows, I think, that the notion of a practice is essentially the notion of a way of acting. Some practices, for example, the ones I (and Wittgenstein) have used as examples, involve finding things out (like color-facts, name-facts, history-facts). Other practices, like walking or driving a car, are not verbal practices or symbol-using practices, and they do not involve finding things out. But all practices involve an ungrounded way of acting. That ungrounded way of acting *can* be represented in sets of propositions ("The floor will support me" "The world has existed for centuries") if we become self-conscious about such practices. It is a mistake, however, to regard such a proposition as defective when it cannot, in turn, be found out (grounded). To demand this is to sever it from its role in determining action.

This point has obvious and important consequences for epistemology. It flies in the face of the demand that all beliefs be justifiable and investigable. The position for which I shall argue (and which is to be found in Wittgenstein) is that this demand is not only unsatisfiable but unintelligible once we understand knowing, believing, and doubting as attributable only to participants in practices.

Parenthetically, there are passages in *On Certainty* in which Wittgenstein seems to lose sight of the priority of action over belief, passages where he seems to refer to "certain propositions striking us immediately as true." He seems to imply, for example, that there are "fundamental principles of human inquiry" (passage 670) and that there are "a lot of empirical propositions" which have the "peculiar logical role in the system" insofar as "we affirm them without special testing" (passage 136).[26] In what sense are there such fundamental and indubitable propositions? Let us distinguish the negative thesis that, even when represented as

---

25. See also passages 109, 110, 148; 345, 346, 358, 359, 427, 472, 476, 510, 559.

26. We can contrast this with passage 248, in which the foundation metaphor is turned on its head:

248. I have arrived at the rock bottom of my convictions. And one might almost say that these foundation-walls are carried by the whole house.

propositions, these matters are not subject to justification, doubt, or grounding from the positive thesis that these propositions are basic knowledge and come to be known in a special way, either as innate notions or as propositions learned and affirmed without question. The positive thesis is an implausible and philosophically unnecessary account of learning once the acquisition of practices is understood. Thus, as Wittgenstein says, it is not a seeing but an acting that "lies at the bottom of the language-game." [27]

Conventionalism   It would be a mistake to infer from this discussion of practices that what we do and what we think are matters of convention. The view that I shall call "conventionalism" involves the following claim. From the view that fundamental beliefs are ungrounded the conventionalist infers that any set of fundamental beliefs and any way of acting (any set of practices) is as unjustifiable as any other way of acting. No fundamental beliefs are to be preferred to alternative beliefs since such a preference cannot be grounded. All, he claims, are "mere conventions."

Conventionalism in this form is a tenable claim only if there are alternative practices, alternatives to fundamental beliefs. But what intelligible way of proceeding is compatible with the conviction that there are no physical objects, or that all calculations are wrong? We may describe particular kinds of pathological behavior as "acting as if he mistrusted all his calculations," but we cannot see such behavior as other than pathological and such practices as other than self-annihilating.

Of course, any practice which involves language involves some conventions. One's usage of particular words and sentences to represent particular ideas and propositions are matters of convention. I can imagine a way of proceeding in which my name is not T. M. and one in which blue objects are correctly called "red." I can even imagine a situation in which I have been miseducated systematically with regard to the prevailing conventions. Moreover, I can imagine a society in which persons use their own names rarely and have nothing like the familiarity with their names that I have with my own, or a society in which persons are familiar with magenta in the "basic" way that I am familiar with red.

27. See also passages 153, 477, 479, 480.

None of these hypotheses sustain conventionalism in an interesting form philosophically. The beliefs, for example, that objects continue in existence unseen, that the earth exists through human history, and that *this* is my hand are not linguistic conventions. The conventions I have just described are conventions about languages and words, not about beliefs and convictions. When we try to represent conventionalism as a theory about beliefs and convictions, it implies that we can imagine alternative practices. In many important respects we cannot do so; we can only imagine defective sets of practices, i.e., ways of living and thinking in which persons cannot think historically, or in which there is no physics, or in which all walk in fear of falling.

The conventionalist thesis has applications not only to conventions of language but also to those systems of thought and practice where alternative ways of proceeding *are* imaginable. Although we cannot imagine proceeding in the conviction that there are no physical objects, we can well imagine ourselves living in ancient Greece and sharing an Aristotelian world-picture. It has been argued that the replacement of one scientific set of assumptions and methods with another set is the replacement of one set of conventions with another.[28] It is also arguable that different moral and religious beliefs represent different sets of conventions. However, this is not a general feature of practices; to say that a practice is not subject to justification is not to say that it is an arbitrary posit taken from among alternative practices.

On deference to authority   Another thesis that might be labeled "conventionalist" is the view that I have my basic beliefs and practices *only* because I have learned them from authoritative teachers and not because

---

28. In *The Structure of Scientific Revolutions* (Chicago: University of Chicago Press, 1962), Thomas Kuhn draws a distinction between "normal" scientific investigations and a change in the governing assumptions, procedures, or "paradigms" which are definitive of the prevailing way of proceeding in investigations. The kind of change of practice which occurs in science is not relevantly a feature of such practices as using names, using color-language, or doing history. Chapter six is indirectly relevant to the subject of differences between Kuhn's analysis of conceptual frameworks and my own.

I have found them to work or to be true, and so forth. In this sense, they are conventions whether or not I can imagine alternatives.

The following passages suggest that Wittgenstein holds this view.

94. ...I did not get my picture of the world by satisfying myself of its correctness; nor do I have it because I am satisfied of its correctness. No: it is the inherited background against which I distinguish between true and false. 160. The child learns by believing the adult. Doubt comes *after* belief.[29]

The view is questioned by Wittgenstein himself when he asks

493. So is this it: I must recognize certain authorities in order to make judgments at all?

The answer is both yes and no. The posited thesis presupposes, misleadingly, that all beliefs are such that either we hold them unquestioningly and continue to hold them because of authority or we have found them out for ourselves. Neither alternative fits the status of the conviction that one may proceed by induction, or that $2 \times 2 = 4$, or that the earth existed. . . . We have not been taught these simply as facts, to be held without ground and justification, nor have we come upon these as a result of investigation.

The issue is more complex. The adult transmits processes and techniques when he teaches calculating or doing history as much as when he teaches chess or baseball; he is not just imparting facts. We saw above that the child's trust in his teacher is not credulous acceptance of fact (passage 235: "That something stands fast for me is not grounded in my stupidity or credulity"). When practices are taught, the learner acquires them from the teacher to *overcome* the relationship of authority and become autonomous. The learner comes to trust his own skills, and trust for the teacher becomes irrelevant. One acknowledges that the earth existed . . . or that $2 \times 2 = 4$ not on authority but as authoritative.

Experience as ground   One felicitous way in which Wittgenstein refers to the role of such convictions as "$2 \times 2 = 4$" and "The earth existed . . ." in our practices is to say that they are the hinges or axes on which the rest of our investigations turn.

29. See also passages 161, 263, 283.

152. I do not explicitly learn the propositions that stand fast for me. I can *discover* them subsequently like the axis around which a body rotates. This axis is not fixed in the sense that anything holds it fast, but the movement around it determines its immobility.[30]

These passages are a warning against a particular interpretation of the autonomy of practices. We saw that one believes, for example, that "the earth existed . . ." not because one has it on good authority or because one has found it out but because our practices—of doing history, of thinking of our personal past and future—depend on this belief. "What stands fast does so, not because it is intrinsically obvious or convincing; it is rather held fast by what lies around it" (passage 144). But we must be warned against saying that these beliefs are therefore "grounded" in or "confirmed" by experience. What would be wrong in saying this?

130. . . . Isn't it experience that teaches us to judge like *this,* that is to say that it is correct to judge like this? But how does experience *teach* us, then? *We* may derive it from experience, but experience does not direct us to derive anything from experience. If it is the *ground* of our judging like this, and not just the cause, still we do not have a ground for seeing this in turn as a ground.
94. But I did not get my picture of the world by satisfying myself of its correctness; nor do I have it because I am satisfied of its correctness. . . .[31]

These passages bear upon the important and elliptical claim that "it is difficult to begin at the beginning, and not try to go further back" (passage 471).

What is wrong with the metaphor of experience as a teacher? Experience does not transmit, ground, or justify the processes of judging. Rather, experience *is* (another name for) the processes of judging. Experience does not instruct persons to derive anything from experience. Rather, persons derive things from experience, from engaging in prac-

30. Compare passages 655, 144; 341, 343.
31. See also passages 131, 434. It may be objected that ungrounded propositions like "2 × 2 = 4" and "My name is T. M." are indeed found out in the acquisition of the relevant practice. I am using the notion of finding out in the restricted sense of using the vehicle of a mastered practice to discover new facts. One rarely finds out one's own name *after* one is well-practiced in using the names of others.

tices. We have successes and failures within judging-practices (practices in which we make judgments), but the game of judging itself is not to be judged, in turn, by its success or failure; we cannot test it and replace it with a more successful game. It is not, in other words, as if experience were a repository of second-order evidence by which to evaluate the practices in which we use and appeal to evidence, for one cannot judge at all without using those very practices.

Two

On Empirical Propositions, Logic, Rules, and Meaning

The concept of a practice involves a conception of the nature of learning and experience that forces us to refine and revise the familiar notions of (1) an empirical proposition and of (2) the logical features of language. Wittgenstein employs this refined usage without making his rules of usage explicit. This chapter has two purposes. The first is to trace out these important consequences of the notion of a practice; the second is to explain Wittgenstein's usage. In doing so, we will consider the relationship of practices to games, and the function of rules in each.

EMPIRICAL PROPOSITIONS

Let us first distinguish contingent propositions from empirical propositions. Contingent propositions (as opposed to necessary propositions) describe states of affairs that may or may not obtain in the world. The proposition is true if the state of affairs obtains but not otherwise. The determination of the truth of a contingent proposition is a matter of determining how affairs stand, not a matter of logic or of definition. It follows that to deny a contingent proposition, unlike the denial of a definition or a logically true proposition, is not to say something necessarily false.

An empirical proposition, on the other hand, is defined epistemologically: an empirical proposition is verified through experience. Its truth is confirmed or disconfirmed in experience. Grounds for disconfirmation of any empirical proposition may in principle be found.

How does Wittgenstein use the term "empirical proposition"? One possibility is that he means "contingent proposition" when he uses "empirical proposition." This hypothesis is supported by the fact that he calls "empirical" such propositions as "My name is T. M." and "I have never lived on another planet," but they are ordinarily neither confirmed nor disconfirmed but held fast in our judging-practices. Accordingly, he says that the truth of some empirical propositions "belongs to our frame of reference" (passage 83) [1] and propositions having the form of empirical propositions "form the foundation of all operating with thoughts (with language)" (passage 401). It fits this hypothesis that Wittgenstein denies that all empirical propositions are verifiable and testable.

109. "An empirical proposition can be *tested*" (we say). But how? and through what?
136. When Moore says he *knows* such and such, he is really enumerating a lot of empirical propositions which we affirm without special testing; propositions, that is, which have a peculiar logical role in the system of our empirical propositions.

This suggestion, however, must be rejected. "Empirical$_w$" (Wittgenstein's use) does not mean "contingent" since "There are physical objects" and "Objects remain in existence when not perceived" are contingent (their negation does not produce a self-contradiction), and Wittgenstein rejects the idea that *these* are empirical propositions.

35. But can't it be imagined that there should be no physical objects? I don't know. And yet "There are physical objects" is nonsense. Is it supposed to be an empirical proposition?—
And is *this* an empirical proposition: "There seem to be physical objects"?

We need an account of "empirical$_w$" whereby it embraces some propositions held fast but not all contingent propositions. I shall argue that the

---

1. Compare passage 124: "I want to say: We use judgments as principles of judgment."

matter is complex and that there are several points to be made in unpacking "empirical$_w$." It is unclear whether Wittgenstein was aware of all of them. What *is* clear is that he admits his own confusion. In passages 398–402 of *On Certainty,* he gives evidence of this. He begins by asking whether it is not the case that one knows "that there is no stairway in this house going six floors into the earth" even when one has never thought about the matter, and whether the fact that one draws appropriate conclusions doesn't *show* that one knows (passages 398–399). He adds, cryptically, "Here I am inclined to fight windmills, because I cannot yet say the thing I really want to say" (passage 400). Wittgenstein uses the example of the stairway to illustrate that "propositions of the form of empirical propositions . . . form the foundation of all operating with thoughts" (passage 401). But he steps back from this, saying that "the expression 'propositions of the form of empirical propositions' is itself thoroughly bad" because such propositions "do not serve as foundations in the same way as hypotheses which, if they turn out to be false, are replaced by others" (passage 402). All this is elliptical and tentative. I shall try to unpack Wittgenstein's meaning.

Let us first scrutinize the example of the stairway. Suppose I discover a hidden trapdoor, one which leads to a stairway going six floors deep into the earth. Will I not say that my hypothesis was falsified? Then why does Wittgenstein deny this is a hypothesis? He has three things in mind, I think. First, the conviction is not a hypothesis insofar as hypotheses are intentionally offered to account for disparate experiences and to be tested by new experiences. The staircase "hypothesis" is not even thought at all. Second, the claim in 398 is seen as investigable but hardly worthy of investigation. (Perhaps this may be said of some hypotheses.) Third, in ordinary circumstances I will regard the matter of the stairway not as a matter for testing but as a matter held fast in testing other propositions. Told of such a stairway, I may question the veracity of my informant. A comparable example is this. I judge whether letters in my mailbox are mine by whether they are addressed to T. M., but I do not check whether my name is T. M. by examining the letters in my mailbox. And I can imagine unusual circumstances in which I would do the opposite.

With these examples in mind, we can try to elicit the important point of the following remarks.

5. Whether a proposition can turn out false after all depends on what I make count as determinants for that proposition.

318. "This question doesn't arise at all." Its answer would characterize a *method*. But there is no sharp boundary between methodological propositions and propositions within a method.

Wittgenstein follows this up by paraphrasing 318 to say that there is "no sharp boundary" between propositions of logic and empirical propositions, or between rules and empirical propositions (passage 319). He concludes that "any empirical proposition can be transformed into a postulate—and then becomes a norm of testing," (passage 321) but adds, "I am suspicious even of this. The sentence is too general. One almost wants to say 'any empirical proposition can, theoretically, be transformed, . . .' but what does 'theoretically' mean here?" (ellipsis is part of quote).

The examples of the stairway and the mailbox show how a contingent proposition can be treated in ordinary cases as a matter held fast in testing and as a rule for testing other propositions. Whether it makes sense to do so will depend on context: in the absence of amnesia or some other exceptional circumstance, it would be irrational to doubt my name on receiving a letter addressed to my neighbor. It follows that the remark in passage 321 is, as Wittgenstein says, too general: I cannot transform an empirical proposition into a postulate at will. It is not up to me "what I make count as determinants for a proposition," passage 5 notwithstanding. Accordingly, "what is a telling ground for something is not anything I decide" (passage 371). If a proposition expresses a matter to be tested, it does so by virtue of its context. My understanding of the context determines what will count as determinants of truth and falsity.

Wittgenstein is unclear about his main point. It is confusing to say that rules and empirical propositions merge or lack a sharp boundary. Rather, the point is that a proposition is one or the other only in a context and not in vacuo. In context it will be clear (i.e., this is how the practice is carried out) that "My name is T. M." is a rule of testing and "This letter belongs to me" is a proposition to be tested. Of course, a participant may be wrong about whether a particular situation is aberrant and whether an ordinary rule for testing can be used as such. It is also possible that experience may be so completely aberrant that one may not know *what* to treat as a rule for testing at all.[2]

There are really two points here. First, it is always possible to adhere to an ordinary rule of testing in the face of recalcitrant evidence, and one is ordinarily well-served by persevering in this way. Second, it is at the same time possible to imagine cumulatively recalcitrant experiences that make judging impossible. Wittgenstein emphasizes the first possibility when he says that "if something happened to make me doubtful of my own name, there would certainly also be something that made the grounds of these doubts themselves seem doubtful" (passage 516). But he also considers the second: "might it not be possible for something to happen that threw me entirely off the rails, . . . that made the most certain thing unacceptable to me?" (passage 517).

It seems to me that Wittgenstein ignores a third possibility. I may abandon a rule of testing if experiences cohere around a new rule of testing that explains why the old rule is to be modified or abandoned. Passage 516 notwithstanding, if more and more evidence came to light of my being mistaken about my name (decisive long-suppressed evidence of abduction at the age of one), I would be unreasonable to retain my old belief.

The first general point which has emerged from the discussion of empirical$_w$ propositions is that a proposition, as in the examples, may be testable in one context and a rule for testing in another. An empirical$_w$ proposition, then, is testable in at least some contexts. A second and altogether different point, which arises in those passages where empirical$_w$ propositions are contrasted with so-called methodological propositions and propositions of logic, is that certain propositions masquerade as empirical$_w$ propositions but are indeed not testable in any context. Examples are "There are physical objects" and "Objects continue in existence when unperceived."[3] These are pseudoempirical$_w$ and are properly called

2. These considerations are discussed at some length in chapter six.
3. It may be said that these are not propositions at all *because* they are not testable in any context *or* because we cannot experience circumstances in which they are false. It is clear that Wittgenstein suggests such a view in *Philosophical Investigations*. *On Certainty* is more problematic. Such passages as 136, 319, and

"methodological." No doubt about such propositions can exist in any context if certain judging-practices are to be possible. This is a logical and not a psychological or empirical feature of such practices as doing history or doing physics. The syntactical similarity of "There are physical objects" and "There are yellow dogs" may mislead one into regarding both as empirical_w propositions.[4]

Wittgenstein alludes to these distinctions, and to further difficulties in making them, when he asks,

673. Is it not difficult to distinguish between the cases in which I cannot and those in which I can *hardly* be mistaken? ...[5]

"My name is T. M." is a proposition about which I can *hardly* be wrong (ordinarily). "There are physical objects" is a proposition about which I cannot be wrong. This is not a matter of context dependence but of the character of all imaginable experience. To summarize, (1) empirical_w propositions may be treated as rules of judgment in some contexts (and in every context one or another proposition dubitable in other contexts is held fast), and (2) methodological propositions masquerade as empirical_w propositions but are never dubitable or testable. (There are examples which, as anticipated in passage 673, are hard to classify. What about "I have never lived in another solar system"?) In the next sections, empirical_w propositions are referred to as empirical propositions.

Mistake and mental disturbance   Not every wrong belief, conviction, or claim is a mistake. The observation that not all empirical (and relevant) propositions are testable in every context allows us to explain when an aberrant performance is not a mistake.

Wittgenstein points out that there are situations in which mistakes are ruled out because we cannot understand the relation of a speaker to his error. For example, a friend who claims erroneously that he has lived

---

308 suggest to me that Wittgenstein regards these propositions as propositions by some other criterion than falsifiability or testability—and certainly the view that a proposition may be meaningful in a context in which it is not testable or falsifiable seems hard to deny.
4. Compare passage 35.
5. This passage and the distinction it raises are the topics of chapter five.

"for a long time in such and such a place" is, Wittgenstein suggests, not making a mistake but, one must suppose, suffering from a mental disturbance. He concludes that a mistake must have a ground as well as a cause, which is to say that "when someone makes a mistake, this can be fitted into what he knows aright" (passages 67, 71, 74).[6] This means, I take it, that to call such an aberrant performance a mistake, one must know not only that the claim is wrong but also (1) how the person making the mistake might have *gone* wrong and (2) that the person making the mistake was capable of proceeding to the corresponding non-mistaken claim. That is, the steps leading to a mistake must be understandable as the steps of a practice. To say that a mistake must have a ground is to say that he who makes a mistake must have a reason for his mistake. In other words, a wrong claim with regard to a matter ordinarily held fast rather than testable in a particular context (like one's own name or the language in which one is speaking) is not a mistake.

Some comments are needed about what Wittgenstein means by *mental disturbance* since he fails to distinguish two senses. The first sense is illustrated by paranoia. The claims of the paranoiac are systematically wrong because he has eccentric and unrealistic ways of interpreting evidence. Unwitting strangers are seen as intending to do him harm. Treating such mental disturbances involves undoing the patient's procedures by changing his assumptions—assumptions that he holds fast. (Such procedures may be undone and reconstructed in part by tracing their origins in particular learning situations.) [7] The kind of mental disturbance I have in mind is a functional disorder.[8]

A different sense of the notion seems closer to what Wittgenstein has in mind. If I am wrong about my own name, I am likely to be wrong about much else. What is called into question is my capacity to reach

6. See also passages 70, 72, 73.
7. There are, of course, various techniques for treating functional disorders and various theories about treatment. Psychoanalytic techniques are familiar ones which involve the reconstruction of learned practices by tracing their origins. Behavioral techniques, on the other hand, overlay existing patterns of behavior with new ones.
8. I am indebted to Dr. Roy Schafer for suggestions about material in this paragraph and the next.

conclusions, not merely my specific assumptions and procedures in reaching conclusions. This is exemplified by organic rather than functional disorders. Not knowing one's own name, not being able to say what is true, is not a different way of proceeding but a defective way; it is the relative absence of skills. A difference between functional and organic disorder is that in the former the judgment that A is mentally disturbed is often a judgment not only that A cannot do various things but also that A's paradoxical achievement of incapacity itself has grounds.[9] Wittgenstein's view seems to be the simpler one of mental disturbance as defect.

Two further points: (1) A disturbance of the first kind may in practice be hard to distinguish from a genuine disagreement about the existence and interpretation of evidence. The apparent paranoiac may in fact have enemies, etc. Persons with unusual political beliefs are not per se disturbed. (2) Can mental disturbance be manifested by the denial of what I have called "methodological propositions," for example, a denial that objects exist or that they continue in existence unperceived? Such claims may, diagnostically, be important metaphors for the patient's self-conception or self-orientation to the world. But it is not clear that they are, except in an attenuated sense, beliefs or claims at all.

The metaphor of the riverbed By noting the insights and infelicities in the following extended metaphor for practices that involve claims to know, we can extend our general understanding of practices and of the notion of an empirical proposition.

96. It might be imagined that some propositions, of the form of empirical propositions, were hardened and functioned as channels for such empirical propositions as were not hardened but fluid; and that this relation altered with time, in that fluid propositions hardened, and hard ones became fluid.
97. The mythology may change back into a state of flux, the river-bed of thoughts may shift. But I distinguish between the movement of the waters on the river-bed and the shift of the bed itself; though there is not a sharp division of the one from the other.
98. But if someone were to say "So logic too is an empirical science" he would

9. This statement is controversial within psychological theory. I shall not discuss it here since little of my argument depends on it.

be wrong. Yet this is right: the same proposition may get treated at one time as something to test by experience, at another as a rule of testing.

99. And the bank of that river consists partly of hard rock, subject to no alteration or only to an imperceptible one, partly of sand, which now in one place now in another gets washed away, or deposited.

These points are familiar. An empirical proposition may, we have seen, be treated at one time "as something to be tested" and at another as a "rule of testing." Because context matters, we can make no "sharp division" apart from context between tested propositions and rules of testing. And some empirical propositions, the proposition that I have two parents for example, seem subject to no alteration in any anticipatable circumstances; at the same time, I can tell a consistent, if not very credible, story in which even these are false. Finally, some rulelike propositions, like "The earth existed . . . ," characterize my procedure in thinking of the past even though I have not learned them explicitly as rules (passage 95).

An imperfection in the riverbed metaphor is the implication that all that is "hard rock" may be gradually and "imperceptibly" eroded. This is to claim that all propositions which are held fast are homogeneous at least in this respect. To see how much of an oversimplification this is, consider four examples, all drawn from the practice of doing history. The first example is a historical fact that is grounded in evidence, and for which I can find additional evidence, but that is so well-grounded and generally held that it can be said to be held fast as a rule of testing. An example is the proposition, "George Washington was the first president of the United States." I would dismiss out of hand a reference book that denied it. This sort of belief cannot be "gradually eroded." I can give credence to putative counterevidence only at the cost of discrediting most of my beliefs about American history *and* many seemingly unassailable resources. In terms of the metaphor, such a piece of hard rock cannot gradually be transformed to sand and gradually erode.

A second example, important only in contrast to the first, is a hard-rock historical fact (hard-rock because unquestioned and unchallenged) which may be eroded by "normal" evidence. An example is the fact that Adlai Stevenson died of a heart attack in 1965. We may conceive of evidence, such as evidence of poisoning, that may gradually erode this conviction but that will leave other beliefs intact.

A third example is not so much a fact discovered within history as a fact about history and a constraint on the investigation of history. Consider the observation that the American Constitution is best understood as the realization of the conscious and unconscious economic motives of the founding fathers. This may be a matter debated among historians, debated at least in part by resort to evidence, but it is not at the mercy of evidence in the way that the first two examples are. Such matters are methodological principles which characterize different schools of thought and which ultimately may involve different conceptions of the purposes and resources of history. An individual's methodological convictions may be eroded by his discoveries, i.e., by the testing of his theories in application, but such erosion is hardly analogous to the erosion of such facts as the second example.

My fourth example is like the third and unlike the first and second in being a fact about history and a constraint on the doing of history. Even less than the third example is it a fact discovered within history. I have in mind the familiar example of the conviction that the earth existed 100 years ago as this example is used by Wittgenstein. It is hard to see how it could ever be *eroded*, imperceptibly or not.

The riverbed metaphor tempts us to take a similar view of all four examples insofar as they are matters which are held fast. It should now be clear why this is unhelpful. The first example is obviously very different from the second. A conviction held fast may be relatively unconnected with other convictions about historical facts and dependent on relatively isolated pieces of evidence. This is so in the second example and not in the first. An isolated belief *may* be eroded gradually as counterevidence increases *or* negated suddenly in a single discovery, and this is not a function just of how *closely* held the conviction is but of other characteristics as well. As we move from examples of the second kind to examples of the first kind, it becomes harder to see how such convictions, like hard rock, can ever be eroded gradually.

The third and fourth examples suggest still other complexities. The third represents a conviction about how to proceed in doing history. If this, too, is a proposition held fast by historians, it is certainly not one that is simply eroded piecemeal by mounting counterevidence. And the fourth example reminds us not to confuse propositions held fast in some contexts (the stairway example, the Stevenson example) with propositions held fast in all contexts because they "describe" the enterprise.

It may be argued that the fourth kind of example is not at all what Wittgenstein has in mind in the riverbed metaphor.[10] It will be said that, for him, this is not a "hardened" empirical proposition, and indeed not an empirical proposition at all. The argument is weak for two reasons. (1) There is no reason to think that "The earth existed . . ." does not describe the "world-picture," as Wittgenstein uses the notion. (2) If he were, ex hypothesi, to exclude such propositions from the set of those which describe the world-picture and are therefore analogous to a riverbed, his metaphor would be per se defective and incomplete.

It is important to distinguish the four kinds of examples of hard-rock propositions for one further reason. It may be said in criticism of the distinction between the third and fourth examples that there are no certainties that are ultimately immune to challenge. Propositions like "There are physical objects" are, on this view, either disguised tautologies or very general and abstract theories, which may in the end be given up. The view is that these propositions are to be seen as what Thomas Kuhn calls "scientific paradigms," programmatic principles and procedures like those which are identified with Newton's laws of motion or Einstein's law of relativity. The invulnerability of such a paradigm is, according to Kuhn, a necessary heuristic illusion.[11] That is to say, scientists concede that they will at some point have to modify their most general theories, but their proceedings in "normal science" require them to hold paradigms fixed.

This assimilation of Wittgenstein to Kuhn overlooks important features of scientific paradigms. Working within a paradigm, scientists nonetheless conceive of discovering recalcitrant cases and expect the paradigm to be confirmed by experience. The paradigm will be abandoned only as a last resort and only if no simpler accommodation of re-

10. In the rest of this section, I take up again some aspects of the question of Wittgenstein's view of so-called a priori knowledge. This discussion foreshadows the fuller discussion of these matters in chapter five.
11. Compare note 17, chapter one.

calcitrant phenomena is at hand. "Objects do not cease to exist when unperceived," on the other hand, is an example of a proposition for which one cannot in principle speak of counterevidence or of recalcitrant experience.

Note that this assimilation of Wittgenstinian practices to Kuhnian paradigms flies in the face of Wittgenstein's own statement of the riverbed metaphor. Hard-rock propositions "form the foundation of all operating with thoughts" (passage 401); unlike hypotheses, they may not "turn out to be false" and be "replaced by others" (passage 402). He appeals to such examples as "This object will not disappear when I turn my back" (passage 314) and "My body has never disappeared and reappeared again after an interval" (passage 101). Propositions (like scientific paradigms) that are provisionally held fast are to be distinguished from propositions that are inherently exempt from disconfirmation. Both are constitutive of activities in which persons speak of evidence, confirmation, and refutation, but only the former are subject to replacement and change over time. The first kind is "empirical"; the second, "methodological."

LOGIC

What is a proposition of logic? Clearly not all methodological propositions are propositions of logic. Even more clearly not all (or any?) propositions held fast in some contexts (empirical propositions) are propositions of logic. And yet Wittgenstein, in passages we have examined, seems to use "propositions of logic" and "rules" interchangeably and uses both to refer *both* to empirical propositions *when* they are being held fast and to methodological propositions. By reflecting on what he seems to mean by "logic" and by "proposition of logic" we shall discover some new features of practices, and we shall anticipate some points about the role of philosophy.

At several points Wittgenstein seems to attempt to define and describe logic in the context of the notion of a practice. He says that the proposition, "What could a mistake here be like!" is a logical proposition because it "describe[s] the conceptual (linguistic) situation," but that it belongs to a "logic that is not used, because what it tells us is not learned through propositions" (passage 51). Moreover, the facts that certain propositions "might be designated as reliable once for all" (passage 48) and that certain evidence "counts as an adequate test of a statement" (passage 82) belong to logic because they belong to the "description of a language-game" (passage 82). Wittgenstein uses familiar examples to show what is and what is not a logical proposition.

56. When one says: "Perhaps this planet doesn't exist and the light-phenomenon arises in some other way," then after all one needs an example of an object which does exist. This doesn't exist,—as *for example* does.... [Wittgenstein's ellipsis]

Or are we to say that *certainty* is merely a constructed point to which some things approximate more, some less closely? No. Doubt gradually loses its sense. This language-game just *is* like that.

And everything descriptive of a language-game is part of logic.

We have seen that the planet claim is investigable and "Here is a hand" is not. Is *this* distinction a logical one? Wittgenstein says that the claim about the second proposition, "I can't be making a mistake," marks a logical difference because it marks a difference in use and role.

We saw also that "I can't be making a mistake about *p*" is translatable in two ways, depending on whether *p* is an empirical proposition held fast (an empirical$_{hf}$ proposition, which is a contextual determination) or whether it is a methodological proposition. An example of the first is "I can't be making a mistake about the fact that here is a hand." An example of the second is "I can't be making a mistake in the claim that there are physical objects." Wittgenstein would call both of these propositions "logical propositions" because they describe the role of propositions in the language-game (the practice). Note, however, that " I am certain that here is a hand" is not a logical proposition when "Here is a hand" is not held fast, e.g., when it means that I have a preponderance of convincing evidence that the pink object in front of me is a hand and not a plastic imitation.[12]

12. It may seem odd to say that logical status is context dependent, that is, a feature not of propositions but of propositions in context. "I have two hands" has its characteristic logical role in normal contexts and in most contexts—and this involves the feature that I can't be making a mistake about it. To say that it has the feature in ordinary contexts is to say that a special context is required for the

It seems that "Here is a hand" and "My name is T. M." are not *themselves* logical propositions. According to passages 51 and 56, logical propositions are propositions that describe other propositions, particularly with reference to their role. They are metapropositions, for example, "I can't be mistaken about *p*." They may, as in this example, be first-person propositions, but they are generalizable: if it is true as a matter of logic that I cannot be mistaken in the claim that here is a hand, then it is true of anyone (situated as I am situated) that, as a matter of logic, he cannot be mistaken about this claim.

100. The truths which Moore says he knows, are such as, roughly speaking, all of us know, if he knows them.

Such a logical proposition as "I can't be mistaken about the fact that *this* is turquoise" can be wrong in two different ways. First, it may be wrong for logical reasons: I may not be entitled to give the claim a logical status, which I claim it has. Second, I may simply be mistaken in identifying *this* as turquoise. Of course, when "I can't be mistaken about the fact that this is turquoise" is not intended as a logical proposition (i.e., when it means "I have sufficient evidence," or "I can see no reason to think I might be making a mistake," or "I am qualified to rule out the possibility of mistake"), it can only misfire in the second way.

Consider three additional points about the "practice" conception of logic.

1. In passage 43, Wittgenstein seems to consider whether logical propositions are redundant. He notes that "We *cannot* have miscalculated in $12 \times 12 = 144$" is a proposition of logic and asks whether it is not "the same, or doesn't it come to the same, as the statement $12 \times 12 = 144$?"

If the first proposition *is* the same as the second, then both (or neither) are logical propositions. On the other hand, the two propositions are

---

claim that it lacks this particular role; only special kinds of special accounts will be understandable. There are really two points here. First, with regard to a practice (any practice), some proposition or other has to be utterly unproblematic and nonhypothetical in an instance of the practice. This is a logical condition of having and carrying out a practice. The second point is that some propositions and not others characteristically have this role for most instances of the particular practice.

presumably not the same if they have different uses, specifically, if the first (the metaproposition) has uses that the second lacks. In chapter seven, I shall argue that philosophical contexts are one kind of context in which metapropositions have a distinctive role. But without looking at the elusive notion of a philosophical context, we may object that the redundancy theory would in general make it impossible for us to describe our practices in a metalanguage, whether or not it is the distinctive job of philosophy to do this.[13] Wittgenstein himself suggests this distinction when he says that it makes a difference "whether one is learning in school what is right or wrong in mathematics, or whether I myself say that I cannot be making a mistake." In the latter case, in the metaproposition, "I am adding something special to what is generally laid down," adding a logical point about the (logical) role of the proposition (passages 664, 665).

628. When we say "Certain propositions must be excluded from doubt," it sounds as if I ought to put these propositions—for example, that I am called L. W.—into a logic-book. For if it belongs to the description of a language-game, it belongs to logic. But that I am called L. W. does not belong to any such description. . . .

It follows that "We cannot have miscalculated in $12 \times 12 = 144$" adds "something special" to what is "generally laid down" by such propositions as "$12 \times 12 = 144$." What is added is a description of the practice, or in Wittgenstein's words "a description of the language-game." A logic-book would include "I cannot be mistaken about $12 \times 12 = 144$" and not "$12 \times 12 = 144$."

Obviously such a logic-book would include some propositions of the form "I can't be mistaken about . . ." whose meaning and truth are context dependent and some others of the same form whose meaning and truth are not context dependent. In the first case "I can't be mistaken about . . ." (or "I am certain that . . .") would be translatable as " '. . .' is an empirical$_{hf}$ proposition"; in the second it would be translatable as " '. . .' is a methodological proposition."

13. Note that one might hold a redundancy theory of *truth*, for example, without holding a general redundancy theory about metapropositions. There is nothing in *On Certainty* about redundancy theories of truth.

2. Such a theory of translation may or may not be offered as a way to revise language to disambiguate such propositions as "I am certain that. . . ." It is clear that "I know that . . ." may be used with the same ambiguity as "I am certain that. . . ." What may not be clear is whether Wittgenstein in his remarks about knowing and being certain is advocating a revision of this kind.

According to a nonrevisionist theory, "I know that (or am certain that, or cannot be mistaken that) this is my hand" is in ordinary usage a different kind of proposition from "I know that Napoleon courted Josephine." The first is about the status of the proposition "This is my hand," whereas the second is a claim that I am specially qualified to give grounds for "Napoleon courted Josephine."

252. ... [I]t isn't just that *I* believe in this way that I have two hands, but that every reasonable person does.

On a revisionist theory the first proposition is not in order and is to be replaced with what is explicitly a logical proposition, explicitly a meta-proposition. Wittgenstein seems to commend such a revisionist view, at least for logical propositions of the form "I know that . . . ," when he says that in a logical (or "grammatical") proposition of this form, the " 'I' cannot be important" since the proposition *properly* means that there can be no doubt in such cases. Since " 'I do not know' makes no sense in this case . . . it follows . . . that 'I *know*' makes no sense either" (passage 58). It seems to me that Wittgenstein offers a revisionist theory of "I know that . . ." but not of "I am certain that . . ." or "I cannot be making a mistake that. . . ." [14] The reason *seems* to be that he wants to demarcate special uses for which "I know that . . ." is in order. At the same time, he has no particular concern with disambiguating "I am certain that. . . ." This places him in the inconsistent position of holding that "I know that . . ." makes sense only when "I do not know that . . ." would also make sense. But he does not have the same scruples about "I am certain that . . ." or "I cannot be making a mistake that. . . ." They make sense in situations in which "I am not certain that . . ." and "I can be making a mistake that (or about) . . ." do *not* make sense. In other words, only the latter

14. See passages 100, 112, 389, 11, 12.

two locutions and not "I know . . ." are appropriate for logical propositions according to Wittgenstein.

3. There are echoes of Wittgenstein's *Tractatus*[15] in the following remark.

501. Am I not getting closer and closer to saying that in the end logic cannot be described? You must look at the practice of language, then you will see it.

The claim that logic cannot be described is puzzling. Does not the theory that logical propositions are metapropositions about propositions and their role in practices "describe" logic? Consider two alternative explanations of passage 501.

1. Because the logical status of some propositions is context dependent, a complete logic-book would have to be a complete account of those contexts in which such propositions are held fast and those contexts in which they are investigable. But then a logic-book would have to describe every possible move in every possible linguistic practice. Logic in this view is not a set of principles but a complete account of every practice involving language. To do logic is to be self-conscious about all the possible uses of language.

The kinds of propositions that have analogous roles in different practices—calculating, doing history, using names—are irreducibly heterogeneous.

213. Our "empirical propositions" do not form a homogeneous mass.

To identify a proposition as one held fast for purposes of a language-game is simply to be able to play the game as an initiate. No putative principles that "describe logic" could allow the identification and isolation of propositions held fast without the unending identification and isolation of contexts as well.

2. For Wittgenstein, the propositions of logic describe "the language-game" (passage 56), the "conceptual situation" (passage 51), or simply linguistic practices. Propositions of logic do not describe logic. For this, would metametapropositions be required, offering a characterization of

---

15. *Tractatus Logico-Philosophicus,* trans. D. F. Pears and B. F. McGuiness (London: Routledge, Kegan Paul, 1961), sections 4.121–4.1213.

the status of metapropositions? What would such metametapropositions look like? Consider some possible candidates.

(a)   I cannot be wrong that this is red.
(a₁) "This is red" is an empirical proposition used as a rule for testing.
(b)   I cannot be wrong about the fact that I cannot be wrong that this is red.
(b₁) " 'This is red' is an empirical proposition used as a rule for testing" is either a methodological proposition or an empirical proposition used as a rule for testing.
(b₂) "I cannot be wrong that this is red" is either a methodological proposition or an empirical proposition used as a rule for testing.

(b) is an attempt to formulate a metaproposition describing the role of (a), which, as translated by (a₁), is itself a logical proposition. (b₁) and (b₂) are attempts to make the logical characterization in (b) explicit. An informal rendering of (b) is that such observations about the roles of propositions in my practices are not the *sorts* of matters about which I can be wrong, or at least that this particular observation about the role of a proposition is not the sort of thing about which I can be wrong. That is, (b) describes a linguistic practice just as (a) describes a practice, but (b) describes a different practice, the practice of reflecting self-consciously about practices. There seems to me no reason to deny that propositions like (b) describe logic.

RULES AND THE METAPHOR OF GAMES

We have already encountered the notion that some empirical propositions are used as *rules* of judgment and that some practices are to be called "language-*games*." In each practice we have considered—using color words, calculating, doing history, learning physics—it makes sense to speak of some relevant technique or other which must be mastered as one becomes a participant in the practice. In this section I shall consider analogies and disanalogies between games and practices.

In games like chess and baseball, one is instructed by the rules to act in certain ways. Certain other ways of acting are not available under the rules and may explicitly be forbidden. One plays chess or baseball insofar as one submits to rules. A player does not treat the fact that the bishop moves diagonally as a fact about the world to be taken on authority but as a way in which he must treat the bishop if he is to be able to play chess.

Analogously, we have seen that "This is red," "My name is T. M.," and "The world existed 100 years ago" are not learned as authoritative facts but are to be regarded as bases for action, as rules to follow if one is to speak of colors, use names, or do history. I am, as it were, instructed to treat these objects as red, these experiences as experiences of redness; I am instructed to treat my name as T. M. in sorting mail, responding to questions, etc. If I am to do history, I must treat the world as if it existed 100 years ago—and well before that.

The metaphor of games also explains the nature of mistakes in acting. The child who moves pieces at random is not making a mistake when he moves the knight diagonally. Similarly, the very young child who emits the sound "red" in the presence of a blue ball has not necessarily made a mistake. To be able to make a mistake one must be an initiate in the practice, must be capable of doing things "aright." [16] Being qualified as a participant in the practice, whether chess playing or doing historical research, is not so much a matter of following the rules correctly in each application as a matter of having learned and being able to engage in that kind of activity. (In chess one uses the notion of mistake for simple violations of rules *and* for errors of strategy. In the latter case what is or is not a mistake may be a matter of controversy. Similarly, some mistakes of historians will be simple mistakes, misreadings of texts perhaps, and others will be controversial matters of strategy and approach.)

Persuasive as it is, the analogy between games and practices, and between propositions that are like rules and rules themselves, is misleading in several important ways.

1. An obvious difficulty is that in games the distinction between rules and moves which implement rules is usually clear. The rule governing movement of the bishop is not a move within the game. I cannot be wrong about whether a proposition describes a rule or a move.

16. Compare passage 74: "Can we say: a mistake doesn't only have a cause, it also has a ground? I.e. roughly: when someone makes a mistake, this can be fitted into what he knows aright."

The same does not hold for practices, as we have seen.

98. ...the same proposition may get treated at one time as something to test by experience, at another as a rule of testing.
309. Is it that rule and empirical proposition merge into one another?

I can, arguably, be mistaken about whether (in special circumstances) my name is to be tested by looking at the contents of my mailbox, or vice versa. To be sure, *some* rules of the practice, those which I have called "methodological propositions," are never to be tested. But clearly some rules of doing history, to take another example, do vary with context, are challenged on evidentiary grounds, and remain controversial.

2. The second disanalogy is closely related to the first. I can specify the rules of chess or baseball more or less exhaustively. But can I even begin to do this for the activity of doing history, or of using names, or of calculating? The rule that objects are to be regarded as continuing in existence when not perceived is not, it seems, a rule of chess or baseball but of the context in which such games occur. Is it a rule of history, because Napoleon, for example, is thought of as existing unseen, or a rule of some more encompassing practice, which includes history? What about the rule that the earth is to be treated as having existed throughout human history? Is *this* a rule of history?

There are several problems here. First, the rules of a practice are not delimitable as are the rules of a game like chess or baseball. Second, the rules of a practice are not fixed and analytically identified with the practice as the rules of chess, for example, are identified with chess. There are (obviously) many schools of history and many ways of proceeding. Third, practices overlap other practices and the outlines of a particular practice must be drawn more or less arbitrarily. Are history and political science, as currently practiced, the same, different, or overlapping practices? The question cannot be answered, unlike the question whether baseball and poker are different practices.[17] Finally, practices seem to be

17. Strictly speaking, these distinctions seem to be matters of degree. One might say that baseball and chess overlap insofar as they have rules in common, like the rules that players compete to win and take turns. It is clear, however, that the distinctions are evident and that the suggestion that they are the same practice or overlapping ones is otiose. The same can be said of the suggestion that they are embedded within the larger practice of playing games.

embedded within other practices: doing history includes the practices of doing research, writing narratives, etc., and is included within the larger practice of understanding and describing reality.[18]

3. The problem is compounded by still another set of difficulties. I can learn chess (or for that matter, a new language) in one of two ways. I can read and memorize rules (and books of grammar, etc.), or I can immerse myself in trying to play (being corrected, etc.) and can acquire skill and understanding through acting.

For the activities that Wittgenstein calls "language-games," only the second alternative is available: they are all learned through doing.

95. The propositions describing this world-picture might be part of a kind of mythology. And their role . . . can be learned purely practically, without learning any explicit rules.

They not only *can* but must be learned in this way because "not only rules, but also examples are needed for establishing a practice. Our rules leave loop-holes open, and the practice has to speak for itself" (passage 139).

140. We do not learn the practice of making empirical judgments by learning rules: we are taught *judgments* and their connexion with other judgments. A *totality* of judgments is made plausible to us.[19]

In other words, these "games" can only be learned by performing particular (paradigmatic) moves, as we saw in chapter one. Until I already use some names, I cannot master the art of naming.

Only if I have clear familiarity with some instances of the application of the practice can I understand what circumstances logically exclude a mistake.

26. But can it be seen from a *rule* what circumstances logically exclude a mistake in the employment of rules of calculation?

What use is a rule to us here? Mightn't we (in turn) go wrong in applying it?

27. If, however, one wanted to give something like a rule here, then it would

18. These matters are covered in greater detail in my paper, "The Concept of a Practice," *Philosophical Studies*, vol. 24, no. 4 (1973), pp. 209–226.
19. Compare *Philosophical Investigations*, paragraphs 200 and 201.

contain the expression "in normal circumstances." And we recognize normal circumstances but cannot precisely describe them. At most, we can describe a range of abnormal ones.[20]

We can see the significance of all this by comparing the learning of a second language with the learning of a mother tongue. The second language may be learned by studying rules, the first only by practice. The practices with which we are concerned in *On Certainty* are generally like a first language. It follows, I think, that we can learn games (like chess and baseball) by studying the rules only because we already have something like a first language, a form of life within which moving pieces, having strategies, winning and losing, etc., all make sense as familiar experiences. Chess is learned as a variation of familiar kinds of activities, not as a kind of activity de novo; the same, I think, can be said of all learned games.

This observation forces us to reverse the explanatory strategy sometimes attributed to Wittgenstein. Rather than invoking games with their constitutive rules to explain the possibility of practices and rule-governed ways of proceeding, we need to invoke practices in order to understand the possibility of having games. In other words, the disanalogies we have marked out do not point to the conclusion that the practices of life are defective or deformed games. Rather, such disanalogies point to the conclusion that games are specialized and simplified cases of practices and can be learned and practiced only by those who already have a context of shared activity in practices (shared expectations and thoughts).

Wittgenstein singles out the law of induction as a particularly clear example of a way of proceeding that cannot be learned as a rule of a game. He observes that a person does not appeal to a "universal law of induction" when, in ordinary circumstances, he trusts without confirmation or checking that he has two hands, any more than a squirrel appeals to a universal law of induction to decide that it will need provisions for the winter (passages 133, 287). He asks why we assume there must be "one universal law first, and not the special one straight away" (passage 133), why we assume there must be "some basic principle on which we accord credence" for "what can such a principle accomplish?" (passage 172).

20. See also passages 44 and 45.

In other words, the law of induction is manifested in what we expect, how we think, and what we do; it is not a rule that we have learned in order to play the games of expecting, thinking, and doing.

4. A fourth disanalogy follows from the point just made. The rules of games have alternatives; more importantly, within a certain range the rules are often arbitrary. If the bishop can move diagonally, why not try out a game in which it moves horizontally? If a player can have three strikes in baseball, why not experiment with letting him have four?

Our ways of proceeding in doing history or our procedures in giving names or colors are never seen as arbitrary posits in this sense, although the names and colors themselves are arbitrarily changeable symbols. (The point here is related to the rejection of conventionalism in chapter one.) Some of the most basic "rules" of, for example, doing history have no viable alternatives. I can *say* that I am acting on the "alternative" rule instructing me to *pretend* with others that the world existed 100 years ago, even though I believe the contrary. But how could this belief—and its difference from ordinary practice—come out in what I do? Moreover, when alternative assumptions and strategies *do* exist (as represented by Whig and Marxist conceptions of how to apprehend history, for example), they are not seen by any of the participants as arbitrary choices or inventions.

5. In my practices of calculating, doing history, and speaking of real objects persisting in time, etc., I may represent my rules as propositions that I hold. There *are* physical objects; objects *do* continue in existence, etc. This, as Wittgenstein says, is part of my world-picture. Even if I cannot prove realism, for me to be engaged in these practices is for me to have the attitudes of a realist.[21]

I make no such claims for the rules of games. "The bishop moves diagonally" is true only in the attenuated sense that it is a prevailing and changeable convention of a game. My claims about ordinary games do not present and cannot support the kinds of questions about knowing, doubting, and having grounds raised in *On Certainty*. A game is a much simpler thing than most of the kinds of practices in which we engage and which we must explain; it is a metaphor of limited utility. The dis-analogies we have found all point in similar ways to those limitations.

21. I discuss this in chapter three.

Although every instance of a practice can be seen illuminatingly as rule-governed activity, our behavior is not organized into discrete moves and nonarbitrarily distinguishable games, nor is it learned in the ways games may be learned, by studying rules. A special disability attaches to the phrase *"language*-games" because the relevant behavior is in many practices not exclusively or even predominantly linguistic. Verbal behavior is significant because it is embedded in a context of ways of behaving, a context in which others have anticipatable thoughts and expectations; these are a language only in a metaphorical sense.

ON MEANING

On Certainty contains remarks about meaning and meaningfulness which are part of Wittgenstein's discussion of rules. First, Wittgenstein notes that words and expressions—as sounds and symbols—do not have meaning in themselves but have it insofar as they are used in practices.

601. There is always the danger of wanting to find an expression's meaning by contemplating the expression itself, and the frame of mind in which one uses it, instead of always thinking of the practice. That is why one repeats the expression to oneself so often, because it is as if one must see what one is looking for in the expression and in the feeling it gives one.

He then explicitly connects the fact that words have meaning with the facts that they are used and that *rules* govern use. He says that the meaning of a word is "a kind of employment of it" (passage 61), since one learns the meaning of a word when one learns to employ it. Thus, he connects the concept of meaning with the concept of rules of usage (passage 62).

What views are being opposed here? We saw in chapter one that knowing the meaning of "red" is (in part) typically a matter of using "red" properly and behaving in other ways appropriate to the practice of using color-words. (At the same time, part of the analysis of "knowing the meaning of 'red' " may have nothing to do with behavior, e.g., being able to imagine a red patch.) This claim stands in opposition (1) to the view that using the word properly is only contingently related to knowing the meaning (for if you use it improperly, you do not know the meaning, your protests to the contrary notwithstanding) [22] and (2) to the view that using the word properly is a condition for knowing the meaning, as if knowing were a distinct act with preconditions. (On the other hand, it is correct to say that having evidence of A's using the word properly is ordinarily a condition of attributing to A knowledge of the meaning of the word. It is not a necessary condition, for I may attribute to an adult speaker of English knowledge of the meaning of "chair" without evidence of his use of the word, and it is not sufficient because A may, for example, be a simple automaton, to which we *may* not wish to attribute knowledge at all.)

It follows that one cannot be said to know the meanings of words unless one can be said to be certain of (and to be a user of) propositions that represent paradigmatic uses of the terms.

114. If you are not certain of any fact, you cannot be certain of the meaning of your words either.
126. I am not more certain of the meaning of my words than I am of certain judgments. Can I doubt that this colour is called "blue"? . . .

To be certain of the meaning of "blue" is to be certain of both the meaningfulness and the truth of some propositions in which it is employed.

An important refinement of the point in passage 126 is that one cannot be certain of the truth of a proposition except in a context of use, as we have seen. Thus, by "judgment" in passage 126 we must take Wittgenstein to mean a proposition used in a context. To summarize, a word has meaning as a candidate for use in a proposition which has meaning, and a proposition is meaningful (has meaning) used in a context. The following remarks are concerned with the meaningfulness of sentences and propositions.

347. "I know that that's a tree." Why does it strike me as if I did not understand the sentence? though it is after all an extremely simple sentence of the

22. In other words, my holding some facts to be certainly true is the measure of my understanding them.
  80. The *truth* of my statements is the test of my *understanding* of these statements.
  81. That is to say: if I make certain false statements, it becomes uncertain whether I understand them.

most ordinary kind? It is as if I could not focus my mind on any meaning. Simply because I don't look for the focus where the meaning is. As soon as I think of an everyday use of the sentence ... its meaning becomes clear and ordinary.

469. In the middle of a conversation, someone says to me out of the blue: "I wish you luck." I am astonished; but later I realize that these words connect up with his thoughts about me. And now they do not strike me as meaningless any more.[23]

In these and many other examples Wittgenstein stresses that one can only speak of the meaningfulness of propositions in contexts and not of meaningfulness *tout court*. His reason is that to know the meaning of *p* I must know what would count as grounds for or against *p,* and therefore I must know for what purpose *p* was said and what rules for finding out about *p* are relevant. One example is that if I do not know the point of making a particular measurement, I do not know how much exactness to demand and, therefore, what grounds to use to judge "This is four inches long." In this sense I do not know what is *meant* by "This is four inches long" if I do not know whether it means "This is four inches long (to the nearest eighth of an inch)" or "This is four inches long (to the nearest micron)." Similarly, "This is blue" is meaningful to me only to the extent that the context allows me to determine whether blue is being distinguished from red or from indigo. In general, then, the meaningfulness of a judgment is not determined by the fact that it is well-formed and uses understandable words in familiar ways.

It may be said as an objection that "I am here" and "That is a tree" are meaningful as propositions even when they have no point as utterances, that one may know *what* was said even when one does not know *why* it was said. The objection shows, I think, not that propositions have meaning in isolation from contexts, but that persons are ready and able to project a standard context and standard purpose for many propositions and hypothetical utterances. Propositions have meaning by virtue of that standard context. Assume sentence S is uttered, as in the examples from Wittgenstein, for no obvious purpose. If there is no characteristic usage of S and it is used to make different points (do different jobs), then it

23. See also passages 348, 393, 460, 461, 463, 464, 468.

becomes obvious that meaning depends on context. On the other hand, if there is a typical or characteristic use of S, then S may seem to have meaning *tout court.*

An example of the first kind is "I know that that's a tree." In claiming knowledge, does the speaker claim facility in English, or is he claiming that the object is not an imitation, or that it's not a mirage, or something else? An example of the second kind is "Good morning." We treat this as a greeting and supply the appropriate context. Another such example is "I wish you luck." One knows spontaneously what sort of context is appropriate and what features it must have (e.g., responding by thank- ing) without knowing just why he has been wished luck. And what he knows is not negligible; his ability to entertain hypotheses about why he has been wished luck is predicated on the meaningfulness of the utter- ance to him. Here is still another example. If I deny that grass is green, my hearer may question my veracity, my understanding of what I've said, my ability to speak English, but he will assume a standard context in which what I have said has meaning and he will be in no doubt about what it is that I have denied.

Although I have discussed the relationship between an utterance having a point and an utterance having meaning, I have not said that the point *is* the meaning. The point of an utterance may be to amuse, inquire, express anger, etc., but that is not the meaning. But by virtue of having meaning, the utterance is able to serve its point. To be sure, when per- sons understand the meaning of a proposition by projecting a typical context of use, they understand the proposition as serving, at best, a hypothetical point.

SUMMARY

The observation that propositional utterances are moves within prac- tices has implications for important issues in philosophy of language and the theory of meaning. It implies that the question whether a prop- osition states a testable matter, a matter falsifiable by facts, can only be asked about a proposition in context, where the context is defined in part by the expectations and roles of participants in a practice. Thus, it forces refinement of the notion of an empirical proposition. Questions of logic are raised by these and other questions about the structure of practices and the relationships of propositions to each other and to speakers. Such logical investigations of the structure of practices lead, in turn, to a comparison of practices with games and of propositions used as rules for judging with the rules of games. Finally, an investigation of *meaning* must begin with the concept of a practice and with the observation that words have meaning insofar as they are used to make moves within practices.

Three

On Justification

In chapters one and two I introduced the notion of a practice as a methodological tool for understanding the rule-governed character of human reasoning and action. In this chapter and the next one, I turn from practices in general to what can be called "knowing-games," those practices in which persons make claims to know and engage in finding things out. Among the characteristic moves in knowing-games are justificatory moves.

EXPLANATION AND DESCRIPTION

Let us begin by recalling that some matters are testable only when other matters are held fast. In other words, some matters are in a position to be justified only if other matters do not need justification and are not the proper subjects of justification.

163. Does anyone ever test whether this table remains in existence when no one is paying attention to it?

We check the story of Napoleon, but not whether all the reports about him are based on sense-deception, forgery and the like. For whenever we test anything, we are already presupposing something that is not tested. . . .

Wittgenstein asks whether testing does not "come to an end" (passage 164), and suggests that when testing ends, one passes from "explanation to mere description" (passage 189). To say that testing comes to an end is to say that justification comes to an end (passage 192).[1]

Over and over again, we come up against the distinction between what is testable and what is not testable, between what is to be justified and what is not the appropriate subject of justification. We must not be misled by the form of a contingent proposition into assuming it is always a matter for testing. Note in this context how Wittgenstein uses (in passage 189) the notions of explanation and description. When persons give reasons (grounds) as justification within a practice, this is explanation. The practice itself is described and not explained when its rules are laid forth; at this point, explanation passes into description.

Consider again the practice of investigating history. Many questions are not "real" questions for the practicing historian. He will not wonder whether every report about Napoleon is based on delusion and whether the earth existed 150 years ago. In logically possible contexts these might be real questions. It is logically possible that one might find independent evidence of a perceptual disorder that afflicted most Frenchmen in the early nineteenth century and led them to misdescribe others. It is logically possible that historians may come to place credence in extraterrestrial communications, radically altering the conception of human history.

These examples will help in elucidating what it means to say that justifying is a move that can occur only within a knowing-practice (knowing-game) and that it makes no sense to demand justification for a practice per se. In later parts of this chapter, I shall argue that philosophical doctrines like realism and pragmatism *can* be seen as attempts to give just such a justification, although there are certainly other ways in which they have been and can be used. I shall also look more closely at justification properly so-called. But before doing so, let us lay to rest several possible sources of confusion.

1. Wittgenstein often labels as "nonsense" any utterance in context that is not the proper subject of testing and justification. On this view, the utterance of any empirical$_{hf}$ proposition and of any methodological proposition at any time is nonsense. He even implies that the utterance

---

1. See also passages 186, 188.

of an empirical proposition that is not being used as a rule (or held fast) is nonsense if the proposition seems unassailable.

10. I know that a sick man is lying here? Nonsense! I am sitting at his bedside, I am looking attentively into his face.—So I don't know, then, that there is a sick man lying here? Neither the question nor the assertion make sense. . . .

Utterances can be nonstarters for many reasons. The sounds may not be words; the words may not be well-formed sentences, etc. Wittgenstein is concerned with a special kind of nonsense, that which violates the "logic" of practices, i.e., seeming to make a testable knowledge-claim when the matter at issue seems indubitable.

2. The exclamation "Nonsense!" implies that one may properly say only testable and justifiable things and that all other linguistic moves are nonstarters. Saying what one would have no reason to question or doubt or investigate is a nonmove.

This is obviously too sweeping a claim. It seems correct that these may be nonmoves in the context of a knowing-game. But there are other uses of language; we warn of danger, express pain and love, describe beautiful objects, greet friends, and so forth when there is no question of finding things out and giving grounds. Thus, Wittgenstein's warnings about dubitability and justification are best taken as warnings about knowing-games and not as general strictures about the meaningful use of language.

3. What does Wittgenstein mean by "explanation"? He says that "at some point one has to pass from explanation to mere description." Within knowing-games, a request for an explanation is, for Wittgenstein, a request for grounds. This may involve different kinds of grounds for different claims or for the same claim in different contexts. One may give documentary evidence for historical claims; one may justify the results of calculation by redoing the procedures; one may justify the claim that this is magenta by pointing to a color chart. In each case one moves to support a claim. *If* such moves are to be what one means by "explanation," it is tautologically true that explanation ceases when "justification comes to an end."

This is obviously a technical employment of the term. We commonly talk about explanations that cannot be taken as justifications. If I claim that a conclusion is supportable by certain kinds of evidence and that other kinds are irrelevant, I thereby explain the conclusion within the context of the knowing-game. There is also a sense in which I not only explain conclusions by pointing to the kind of evidence that confirms them but also explain practices as a whole by showing what purposes they serve. For example, I can try to describe what experience would be like without proper names or color-language or reflections about the past. In this expanded (and ordinary) sense of explanation, it is not at all clear that when we move away from giving grounds we thus move from "explanation to mere description."

More generally, there are all sorts of moves in language that are not the presentation of grounds and that are, in a perfectly acceptable sense, explanations. We may explain an utterance by showing how it serves as a warning or greeting. One may explain a "methodological" belief by showing how it enables persons to proceed in practices.

These qualifications do not affect the main point that propositions like "There are physical objects" can *masquerade* as moves within knowing-games when they are at best "mere descriptions." They describe, in Wittgenstein's words, our "world-picture." This main point has by no means been generally conceded in the history of philosophy. When Wittgenstein criticizes realism and pragmatism, he seems to criticize them as two attempts to treat such propositions *as* moves within knowing-games and therefore as attempts to justify such propositions by giving grounds.

Realism   What is wrong with saying that historical beliefs and beliefs about nature (and so forth) are justified *because* they agree with reality? Why can't we say this to justify ordinary beliefs and reject fictive hypotheses? Wittgenstein notes that everything speaks in favor of the "hypothesis" that the earth has existed for a long time, and he asks whether one can conclude that it therefore "certainly agrees with reality?" He concludes that "with this question you are already going round in a circle" (passage 191). The objection, it seems to me, is that there is no test for whether the set of our beliefs agrees with reality any more than there is a test for whether a calculation that has been sufficiently checked is or is not to be relied on.

212. In certain circumstances, for example, we regard a calculation as suf-

ficiently checked. What gives us a right to do so? Experience? May that not have deceived us? Somewhere we must be finished with justification, and then there remains the proposition that *this* is how we calculate.
215. Here we see that the idea of "agreement with reality" does not have any clear application.

When does the idea of "agreement with reality" have no clear application? Does it ever count as justification to say this? I interpret Wittgenstein as offering the following response.

We say that historical facts and the results of investigation in physics, chemistry, anthropology, etc., agree with reality; we are less likely to say that the results of calculation agree with reality, although perhaps we will say to a recalcitrant child, "Seven times eight *is* fifty-six; that's just how things are." One difference between these two kinds of knowing-games is that the first and not the second deals explicitly with material objects. Whether or not any other differences may be picked out as essential, we are sometimes content to distinguish the first set of knowing-games as ones that involve the description of "reality." This is a characterization of knowing-games and not a justification of them. The practice of doing physics no more stands in need of justification than the practice of calculating. It makes sense to say that individual propositions within physics or history agree with reality, and by this we mean that they have been found out by available procedures and that, therefore, we can give grounds for them. But the practice itself is not found to disagree or agree with reality any more than the practice of calculating is found to agree or disagree.

608. Is it wrong for me to be guided in my actions by the propositions of physics? Am I to say I have no good ground for doing so? Isn't precisely this what we call a "good ground?"[2]

Both realism and idealism can be seen from this point of view as incoherent doctrines when they are offered as answers (realism as an affirmative answer, idealism as a negative one) to the question whether or not our knowing-games taken together (our world-picture) agree with reality. The question is a pseudoquestion. The testing of agreement with

2. See also passage 471.

reality cannot go on on this level. The notion of a procedure for testing does not make sense.

24. The idealist's question would be something like: "What right have I not to doubt the existence of my hands?" (And to that the answer can't be: I *know* they exist.) But someone who asks such a question is overlooking the fact that a doubt about existence only works in a language-game. Hence, that we should have to ask: what would such a doubt be like?, and don't understand this straight off.

If the idealist is mistaken in saying that my right not to doubt must be grounded in (unavailable) reasons, the realist is similarly mistaken in claiming to have such reasons.

58. If "I know etc." is conceived as a grammatical proposition, of course the "I" cannot be important. And it properly means "There is no such thing as a doubt in this case." . . .
59. "I know" is here a *logical* insight. Only realism can't be proved by means of it.

The distinction between the position taken in these chapters and realism (on this interpretation) should now be clear. Persons are content to regard some of their knowing-games (physics, history) as activities of finding out about reality; this can't be wrong since it is not an assumption: the things described by physics, history, etc., are part of what is *meant* by the term "reality." It does not follow that realism is true in that it can be *shown* that our knowing-games are the determination of reality. And from the fact that a correspondence (agreement) between our knowing-games and reality cannot be shown (is not the sort of thing that can be shown), it does not follow that idealism is true, if idealism is the view that our beliefs do *not* agree with reality.

At one point (passage 191), Wittgenstein says that I may *designate* a belief in the existence of the earth long before my birth as true. This is misleading. We cannot designate such matters as true or false by will or by choice. The properly stated point is a negative one: when we say that such propositions are true, we do not thereby imply that they have been found out and that we can give grounds for them. They are true in that they are held fast by our investigations.

Several remarks about truth and falsity complement Wittgenstein's discussion of realism and idealism. He says that "if the true is what is grounded, then the ground is not *true*, nor yet false" (passage 205). One can respond to someone who questions the grounds not by *showing* they are true, but by saying "if you learn more you too will think the same" (passage 206). It is not a *reason* for regarding something as "sure evidence" that it is certainly true; that is merely a redescription of the evidence (passage 197).[3]

The point of these remarks seems to be that " 'The earth existed long before my birth' is true" is to be treated like " 'The earth existed long before my birth' agrees with reality." When we say that propositions held fast in investigations are true, we must not stumble into thinking that they too have been found out. Rather, the character of the knowing-game (say, of history) is that it unfolds what is true just as it unfolds the nature of reality. Note however that while it is absurd to say that physics or history "is true" *tout court*, it is not at all absurd to say that propositions held fast like "The earth existed . . ." are true. Those things that are *held* to be true and those that are *found* to be true are subsets of those things called "true."

Coherence and correspondence "theories" of truth each represent partial insights into the use and meaning of the concept. To engage in a knowing-game, to find out how things are, is to see oneself as bringing one's knowing-claims into correspondence with experience (i.e., minimizing recalcitrance). We have already seen that to engage in certain knowing-games is to have the attitudes of a realist. The mode of thinking characterized by correspondence "theory" is one whereby we establish the truth of testable matters by appeal to evidence. On the other hand, correspondence in toto between what we claim to know and the way things are is not itself a matter that can be found out, and it is not a matter that it makes sense to treat as problematical in practice. Thus, with the question "Does it certainly agree with reality?" one is "already going around in a circle."

In this sense, testing involves the mutual coherence of the various things one believes and experiences.

3. See also passages 514, 515.

274. One such is that if someone's arm is cut off it will not grow again. Another, if someone's head is cut off he is dead and will never live again.

Experience can be said to teach us these propositions. However, it does not teach us them in isolation: rather, it teaches us a host of interdependent propositions. If they were isolated I might perhaps doubt them, for I have no experience relating to them.

From this kind of coherence theory, it does not follow that we must or can put aside talk about correspondence.

Pragmatism   A second way in which we may be tempted to justify our world-picture by giving grounds is to say that practices and their underlying beliefs have "proved to pay." These practices are the basis of "outstanding success" in activity and thinking. Wittgenstein sounds like a pragmatist when he says, for example, that the picture of the earth as a ball "proves itself everywhere" (passage 147). And he asks whether we invest belief in geographical, chemical, and historical facts learned in school because proceeding in this way has "proved to pay" (passage 170).[4] Can one say that our practices and procedures are *justified* because they have "proved to pay"? Note that Wittgenstein *disclaims* being a pragmatist. We shall have to explain that disclaimer.

422. So I am trying to say something that sounds like pragmatism.
    Here I am being thwarted by a kind of *Weltanschauung*.

One clue to the reasons for Wittgenstein's rejection of pragmatism lies in those passages, discussed above, in which he distinguishes between the fact that *we* derive judgments from experience and the view that *experience* directs us to derive judgments from experience (passages 130, 131). Similarly, he distinguishes between having a ground from judging and "having a ground for seeing this in turn as a ground" (passage 130), and says that "experience is not the ground for our game of judging [n]or its outstanding success" (passage 131).

474. This game proves its worth. That may be the cause of its being played, but it is not the ground.

4. See also passages 48, 49.

Let us take the *Weltanschauung* of the pragmatist as the view that the ground and justification of our picture of the world is that this picture works better than any alternative picture. To say that about such aspects of experience as "If someone's arm is cut off it will not grow again" or "The earth existed 150 years ago" is to claim to have "a ground for seeing this [experience] *as* a ground" (passage 130), namely, the ground that this picture works better than others. On this interpretation, pragmatism refers irreducibly to a world-picture chosen from alternatives. But a world-picture is not chosen, and it is by no means clear what it means to speak of alternatives. A fortiori, the acquisition of a world-picture is not a *grounded* choice, a choice for which one can give reasons.[5]

To say that our world-picture is not chosen from among alternatives is not to say that we will never be in a position to choose to maintain our world-picture in the face of alternatives. Were we to witness the apparent regrowth of human limbs or to receive apparent evidence of extraterrestrial interference with human thought, we might have grounds for maintaining *and* alternatively rejecting our "old beliefs." In such straits, knowledge *is* "related to a decision" (passage 191), and perhaps a personal one. The decision may be to abandon some familiar practices altogether.[6] But this is not *our* situation. Doing history is not, for us, related to a decision of this kind. The question has not come up, and maintaining our practices in recognizable form depends on its not coming up through recalcitrant experiences.[7] Until and unless there are such experiences, "Perhaps the earth came into being yesterday" is nonsense, not an empirical conclusion rejected for insufficient evidence.

To summarize, we may say of testable propositions that we "accord credence . . . because [they have] proved to pay." We mean by this that we entertain hypotheses within physics and history, for example, as long as

5. Wittgenstein is misleading in this regard when he says, as we have seen, that a proposition which is held fast is not found to be true but "we may designate it as such" (191). Compare 362: ". . . Doesn't it come out here that knowledge is related to a decision?"
6. The kind of decision I am describing is analogous to what Kuhn calls a shift of paradigm.
7. I discuss changes in practices and the understanding of practices in chapter 6.

they are supported by evidence, explain relevant data, and support correct predictions. We may say that they prove to pay as we may say that they agree with reality. In both cases, we indicate in such ways that we can give good grounds. But just as we cannot justify physics or history as an enterprise by showing that it agrees with reality, we cannot justify it by showing that it has proved to pay.

JUSTIFYING AND NEEDING TO JUSTIFY

Justifying, giving grounds, claiming that p is true, claiming to know p, doubting—all are names of moves that occur in knowing-games. But even if we attend to those contexts that involve justification, it is not always clear what is meant by a request for justification or whether such a request is appropriate. The following distinctions are needed.

First, the request for justification within a knowing-game may be ambiguous. It may be, as I have generally interpreted it, a request for grounds for what is claimed, i.e., a showing that p is justified, when the utterance is of the form "p" or "I know that p." It may also be a request for justification of the speech act whereby p is claimed, e.g., a showing that the utterance serves a purpose, does not offend, etc. This is the difference between "I said Mary was kind because she gives to charity" and "I said Mary was kind because I wanted to put her at ease." Only the first example is one of giving grounds for p, "Mary is kind." In what follows I shall be concerned with justification in this sense. (It will ordinarily be clear in context which kind of justification is meant.)

There is an important distinction between *being able* to justify p (in the sense of giving grounds) and *needing* to justify p. I may be able to justify a criticism of George Washington's military strategy both to history students and to colleagues, but I may need to justify p only to the former. One must not, however, confuse this kind of case, in which justification is not needed because it can be taken for granted, with cases in which p cannot be supported because p is more certain than *any* grounds that can be given for it. The latter is a case in which p is held fast. Wittgenstein says, for example, that my having two hands is normally "as certain as anything that I could produce in evidence," and that any grounds that I might *try* to give for my certainty would not be grounds because they would not be "as certain as the very thing they were supposed to be grounds for" (passages 250, 307). Similarly, there are normal situations in which my certainty has this form: "If my memory deceives me *here* it can deceive me everywhere" (passage 506).[8]

507. "If this deceives me, what does 'deceive' mean any more?"

Let us clarify the notion of *being able* to justify (or being able to give grounds for) *p*. The availability of what may be called confirmatory resources is not necessarily the availability of grounds. The possibility of counting my toes is not the possibility of grounding my belief that I have ten toes. I will ordinarily hold fast to the latter even in the face of apparent counterevidence. I am more certain that I use the word "deceive" correctly than I am of anything that a dictionary might say in support. Moreover, I cannot offer you the dictionary as evidence of usage unless I am able to understand your stance as one of doubt, i.e., unless I can understand our shared context as one in which a dictionary definition is more certain for you than your own usage or mine. Being able to justify *p* is therefore not just a matter of having resources that accord with *p* or that in some imagined context might be more certain than *p*. It is a matter of having resources that *are* more certain.

The capacity to recognize some kinds of propositions as more certain than others *is* the capacity to engage in the relevant practice. To need a dictionary in the situations described in passages 306 and 507 is to be unable to engage in the relevant language-game. To mistrust my memory is ordinarily also to be unable to engage in the relevant practice. If I mistrust my memory in certain matters, I will have to give up judging altogether.

632. Certain and uncertain memory. If certain memory were not in general more reliable than uncertain memory, i.e. if it were not confirmed by further verification more often than uncertain memory was, then the expression of certainty and uncertainty would not have its present function in language.[9]

Thus, matters for which no justification *can* be given are to be distinguished from those in which it can be given and is not needed *and* from those in which it can be given and is needed. A very general philosophical mistake is thus uncovered. Descartes held that knowledge is to be

8. See also passage 419.
9. See also passages 115, 280, 329, 450.

gained only by, in principle, doubting everything, by treating everything as testable, but the practical situation is quite otherwise. Knowledge is gained only to the extent that matters dubitable in hypothetical contexts are not doubted but held fast.

392. What I need to shew [sic] is that a doubt is not necessary even when it is possible. That the possibility of the language-game doesn't depend on everything being doubted that can be doubted.

This last sentence is too weak. The point is rather that the possibility of the language-game depends on not everything being doubted that can be doubted.

At the risk of repetition, we can summarize these observations by distinguishing four cases. First, there are cases in which p is neither a matter that can be justified and doubted nor a matter for which corroborating resources can be sought. For example, "There are physical objects" and "Objects continue in existence when not being perceived" express matters that are never matters for testing.

Second, there are cases in which p is not a matter that can be justified and doubted in ordinary contexts but is a matter for which corroborating resources can be found. I cannot doubt or seek to justify that I have two hands or that my words mean what they do or that my name is T. M. without jeopardizing my confidence in my ability to judge at all, except in specific, extraordinary cases. But I *can* nonetheless find my name in my wallet, count my limbs, and check the dictionary.

Third, there are cases in which p is a matter that can be justified and doubted, although there is no need to do so. Ordinarily, "So-and-so told me this, and I believe it to be true" is such a case if so-and-so is truthful and reliable. Another case is "The title stamped on the spine identifies the book bound inside," said without checking in an ordinary context. I can examine the contents; grounds are available to make me more certain, but such checking seems otiose.

Fourth, there are cases in which testing what is questioned and giving justification are appropriate or even necessary moves. To say that there is need to justify p in a particular case is not to say that p will be or ought to be challenged but that it is intelligible as an object of challenge and that the claimant of p claims to be able to produce good grounds.[10]

10. Wittgenstein does not distinguish clearly among these four different kinds of

An account of the structure of the notion of a practice in terms of the justifiability of different kinds of propositions is an analysis of what it is to be reasonable. To participate in a practice in accord with its contextual demands is a way of being reasonable.

252. ... It isn't just that *I* believe in this way that I have two hands, but that every reasonable person does.[11]
324. Thus we should not call anybody reasonable who believed something in despite of scientific evidence.

Knowing-games involve holding some propositions fast, regarding some propositions as testable, and regarding various resources as evidence with certain kinds of reliability. Judging is not just a procedure with a particular form but a matter of believing what one has no reason to question and questioning what one has good reason to question. Being reasonable is not just a matter of acting and thinking in a certain manner or form but also a matter of thinking certain *things*. To think of someone as reasonable is to be able to understand his *reasons;* to understand his reasons is to share the practice within which what he claims to hold as reasons *can be* reasons and what he claims to be able to judge *can be* judged in the way he claims.

---

cases, particularly between the first and second and the second and third kinds. How, for example, are we to treat "I am certain that I have never been in Asia Minor"? This may be of the second or third kind. It is of the second ("If I question this, I impeach my capacities to judge") if I have never been near Asia Minor, never been kidnapped, never had an extended amnesia, etc. It is a case of the third kind if I have traveled near Asia Minor but am comfortably certain (but open to reassurance) that I did not cross the frontier. Here is another example. When Wittgenstein says that "I know a sick man is lying here" is "nonsense" and dismisses "I know that I have two hands" in the same way, he is saying that neither is an appropriate move in a knowing-game. But he does not point out that the reasons in each case are different: the first is of the third kind, for there is no need to appeal to grounds when there is no reason for doubt (e.g., for thinking the man is pretending); the second case is of the second kind since no corroborating investigations could be as certain as the claim itself. A claim like "I know there are physical objects" would be dismissed as "nonsense" for still different reasons since it is a case of the second kind.

11. See also passages 452, 453, 556.

Four

On Knowing and Saying "I Know . . ."

I begin this chapter by assembling tools for use later in the chapter, i.e., by examining some uses of "I know that . . ." and "He knows that. . . ." I then apply my conclusions to Moore's uses of "I know . . ." when he attempts to prove the existence of the "external" world and to refute skepticism. In doing so, I try also to determine Wittgenstein's views about knowing and his criticisms of Moore. The chapter ends with a discussion of the relation between knowing claims and believing claims and with an extension of our conclusions about knowing to believing.

KNOWING AND CLAIMING TO KNOW

There are situations in which I know *p,* in which it may correctly be said of me that I know *p,* and in which it would be pointless for me to claim to know *p.* I may interrupt a discussion of French cooking with the claim, "I know that Kant wrote the *Critique of Pure Reason* before he wrote the *Critique of Practical Reason.*" What I have said is doubly correct; Kant did write the one work before the other, and I do know it. But my saying so is pointless. My claim will be "meaningless" or "nonsense," Wittgenstein suggests, in the sense that my hearers will not have a context for understanding my claim; lacking a context, they will not only find it bizarre but will not know what grounds to use in testing it. Have I, they might think, undisclosed evidence, which casts doubt on the order of Kant's composition? They will ask not only "*Why* has he said this?" but "*What* has he said?" i.e., what position has been taken with regard to what problem or issue?

What is problematic here is not my knowing but my claiming to know. As long as I refrain from claiming to know, *what* it is that I know about this matter is unproblematic for myself and for anyone who happens to know that I know. My claiming to know the order of Kant's work forces my hearers to discount their projection of the obvious and ordinary interpretation of my words (since knowing in the ordinary way cannot be the point of my claiming to know) and leaves them with no other interpretation to put in its place.

These observations are suggested by passages in *On Certainty,* some of which I have examined in different contexts.

464. ... I am sitting talking to a friend. Suddenly I say "I knew all along that you were so-and-so." Is that really just a superfluous, though true, remark? ...[1]

It is not "just a superfluous, though true, remark" because, once it is said, its meaning begins to seem problematic. What evidence is to count for or against? The question of what was said is not independent of the question of why it was said whenever an ordinary and available interpretation of what was said seems to be incompatible with the fact that it *was* said in the particular circumstances.

These remarks help us guard ourselves against the fallacy of *identifying* "A knows ..." with "A is in a position to claim to know. ..." In passage 552, Wittgenstein reminds us that it is certainly the case that one knows he is sitting in a chair even when one will not normally say so. "Even if one doesn't say it, does that make it *untrue*?" (passage 552) He then asks (passage 531) why, if one knows that he is sitting or that this color is called "blue" in English, he cannot describe his state using the words, "I know. ..." Why, in an inappropriate context, does the statement, "I know that I am now sitting in a chair" seem "unjustified and presumptuous" (passage 553)?[2]

Passage 553 yields an important general point. There is no such thing as "simply stating" anything, for example, the truth about my state at a

1. See also passages 412, 413, 481.
2. See also passages 532, 423.

time; all stating is stating for some reason or other (for some expressive or communicative purpose) in some context or other. Understanding what is claimed (or stated) is not independent of understanding why it is claimed and understanding what grounds can be given for it. A knowing claim presumes a context; lacking one, it is presumptuous.[3]

So far, I have tried to distinguish knowing from claiming to know by showing that for a given p (putative object of a knowing claim) there will be cases of knowing p in which claiming to know p is in order and cases of knowing p in which claiming to know p is not in order. It is a separate point that some p's are not putative objects of knowing-claims at all. These are cases in which saying "I know p" is not in order because p is not the sort of thing that anyone in any context can have grounds

---

3. Wittgenstein appends to 532 the following remark: "I do philosophy now like an old woman who is always mislaying something and having to look for it again: now her spectacles, now her keys." The "mislaid spectacles" through which to see the problem of 532 is the point that there is no such thing as simply stating. The following passage does not, as one might suppose, conflict with my account.

> 288. I know, not just that the earth existed long before my birth, but also that it is a large body, that this has been established, that I and the rest of mankind have forebears, that there are books about all this, that such books don't lie, etc. etc. etc. And I know all this? I believe it. This body of knowledge has been handed on to me and I have no grounds for doubting it, but, on the contrary, all sorts of confirmation.
>
> And why shouldn't I say that I know all this? Isn't that what one does say?

One *does* say it, but one says it unproblematically (for one's hearers) only when one's reasons for saying it are transparent. The following passage pinpoints the occasions in which saying "I know . . . " is and is not in order:

> 431. "I know that this room is on the second floor, that behind the door a short landing leads to the stairs, and so on." One could imagine cases where I should come out with this, but they would be extremely rare. But on the other hand I show this knowledge day in, day out by my actions and also in what I say.
>
> Now what does someone else gather from these actions and words of mine? Won't it be just that I am sure of my ground?—From the fact that I have been living here for many weeks and have gone up and down the stairs every day he will gather that I *know* where my room is situated.—I shall give him the assurance "I know" when he does *not* already know things which would have compelled the conclusion that I know.

See also passage 554.

for knowing. Such subjects are what I call in chapter two "methodological propositions." I contrast them with empirical propositions that may be held fast in particular contexts. It is pointless to claim to know an empirical matter when that matter is held fast as a rule in testing (or when it is simply irrelevant, etc.); but it is *generally* pointless to claim to know a methodological matter. An example is "I know that there are physical objects." This is objectionable in a way in which the claim about Kant is not objectionable: whether or not there is a point in my claiming to know that "Kant wrote . . . ," it is correct that I know that "Kant wrote. . . ." It is something that I have learned. But it is not correct that I know that there are physical objects.[4]

Knowing and showing that I know   The distinction between knowing and claiming to know implies that questions about when I can be said to know *p* are ambiguous. They may be questions about (1) when it is true of me that I know *p*, (2) when it is appropriate for me to say that I know *p*, or (3) when it is appropriate for others to say of me that I know *p*.

Suppose it is a correct description of me that I know *p*. What is it that is attributed when I am described as knowing *p*—a mental state, a disposition to behave, a special qualification? Is knowing a matter of behaving in certain ways, or of being disposed to behave in certain ways, or of being in a particular state that may or may not be evinced in behavior? The answer is complex and each of these elements plays a part in it.

Several sections of *On Certainty* offer partial responses to this problem. Wittgenstein asks, "How does a man learn to recognize his own state of knowing something?" (passage 589). His answer is that while one *does* use " 'I know that . . .' [to] say that I am in a certain state" (passage 588), "an inner experience cannot shew [sic] me that I know something" (passage 569). Rather, one can show oneself or others that one knows something by giving other evidence of knowing (passage 432): "That he does know takes some shewing [sic]" (passage 14). Thus, while

4. I shall have more to say about this distinction when I discuss Wittgenstein's critique of Moore.

knowing is not a matter of behaving, it seems to be a matter of being qualified to behave. I shall try to unpack Wittgenstein's position.

An "inner experience" cannot show me that I know p because knowing p is a matter of being *qualified* to do certain things, i.e., to give grounds for p or otherwise give evidence of knowing. But I may know p without in fact *having* to perform, without having to give grounds or other evidence. In this sense, knowing is a state and not an activity. The connection with action is logical and not causal: my knowing p is not the cause of my acting in a certain way (giving grounds, etc.) but is manifested in my acting in a certain way. My failure to act accordingly is not merely evidence that I do not know; in the absence of a relevant explanation of the failure, that failure is tantamount to my not knowing. I may, if necessary, reassure *myself* that I know p in the same way as I can show others that I know p, by engaging in a performance that I am particularly qualified to give and that, by the nature of the practice, counts as a manifestation of my knowing. I can surprise myself just as I can surprise others: failing to give a suitable performance, I may concede that I thought I knew p; having performed suitably, I may admit that I know p and that I thought that I did not. I may claim to know the order of the kings and queens of England; failing to list them, I will say "I thought I knew." Or, I may think that I don't know them, list them nonetheless, and concede that I do know. Even when the performance *seems* like an inner experience, e.g., listing the kings and queens silently to myself, it is important that it is the kind of performance that can easily be made publicly.

There are two different kinds of performance that count, in different contexts, as "other evidence of my 'knowing.'" Suppose I claim to know that the Eiffel Tower is 984 feet high. I may show that I know either by demonstrating that I have used the fact previously *or* by pointing out the fact in a reliable reference work. In the first case, I am showing that *I* know the fact; whether it *is* a fact is not in dispute. In the second case, I show that it *is* a fact and that (incidentally) I know it. In this way, the question "How do you know...?" is ambiguous. The ambiguity is potentially present (and usually eliminated by context) not only when one is asked to justify claims to know *that p*, but also in regard to claims to know *what*, like "I know what that is" (e.g., a zebra) or to claims to know *how*, like "I know how to *q*" (e.g., multiply). In different circumstances, it will be an appropriate supporting action to show *either* that *I* can identify other zebras *or* that the beast before me is indeed a zebra. Similarly, it will be appropriate *either* to show that *I* can multiply (by multiplying) *or* to show that the combinational activities I have performed are indeed what is generally called multiplying. This, as Wittgenstein seems to suggest (passage 588, quoted above), is one difference between "I know that is a zebra" and "That is a zebra." The first, but not the second, can be supported by a demonstration of *my* qualifications.

Knowing: first-person and third-person claims   The distinction between knowing and claiming to know is not only explainable in terms of the distinction between *my* knowing and *my* claiming to know; it is also manifested by the distinction between someone's knowing and my claiming (or being able to claim) that he knows. Wittgenstein intends his remarks to be generalized in this way. He asks, for example, how we are to understand the remark of a forester who assembles his men, picks trees for cutting, and announces, "I *know* that that's a tree" (passage 353). And, in the same passage, he asks us to compare this example with the remark of an observer, "He knows that that's a tree—he doesn't examine it, or order his men to examine it."

The comparison in passage 353 has several implications.

1. In the situation of the forester, it is no more in order for me to say "He knows . . ." than it is for him to say "I know. . . ." Each claim requires a context. "Of course he doesn't examine the tree. Why should he? Do you *mean* that one might think it is a plastic imitation, or a mirage, or . . . ?"

2. There is asymmetry between the forester's claim "I know . . ." and my claim about the forester, "He knows. . . ." The claim "I know this is a sycamore" commits him to showing how it is that *this* has the marks of a sycamore; in some contexts it will suffice to say "I've studied tree classification." On the other hand, my claim "He knows this is a sycamore" commits me to give grounds for believing that he is qualified to claim that this is a sycamore. I am not committed to give grounds for his claim, i.e., to show that this *is* a sycamore. More generally, saying

"I know p" commits him to giving grounds for p but saying "He knows p" does not commit the speaker to giving grounds for p.

3. Since both "I know..." and "He knows..." are offered and testable on the basis of grounds, neither kind of claim is infallible. A third person need not accept first-person testimony either of knowing or of not knowing. A first-person claim may, however sincerely it is made, be corrected by a third-person counterclaim. ("You have convinced me that I do have a reading knowledge of Russian after all.")

The following remarks illustrate this last point. My knowledge of the position of my hands may be immediate, i.e., not grounded in my own observation of myself. But even *this* kind of knowledge is not infallible or immune to correction by others through their observations.

502. Could one say "I know the position of my hands with my eyes closed," if the position I gave always or mostly contradicted the evidence of other people?
504. Whether *I know* something depends on whether the evidence backs me up or contradicts me. ...

Knowing claims: suggested synonyms   One way of eliciting the uses of "I know p" (or "I know that p") is by looking at similar locutions (or suggested synonyms) and comparing their uses with the uses of "I know. ..."

We have seen that "I know that p" implies that the speaker can give grounds for p where p is in question. But the act of claiming p alone also commits the speaker to giving reasons in cases where p is in question. ("It's raining." "Of course it is; anyone can see that." But "The humidity is 93 percent today." "How do you know?") Why then is the claim "I know p" not equivalent to the claim "p"? In some cases the expressions do have the same use. Does this mean that they are interchangeable?

In passage 587, Wittgenstein notes that the one form often does replace the other and that the difference is often a matter of "intonation" or emphasis: one says "I know..." to emphasize certainty or to anticipate being contradicted (passage 591). He concludes, tentatively, that the fact that a person is mentioned in one form and not the other "does not show that they have different meanings" (passage 587). I suggest that one can go further in analyzing the difference.

An important distinction is this: what is *implicit* when I state "*p*" is made explicit when I say "I know that *p*," namely that *I* am a participant in the practice of giving grounds for *p* and that I am qualified to give grounds which will be understood and treated as grounds by others. "How do you know?" may be a request for grounds, *or* it may be a request for credentials, an account of how *I* am qualified to give grounds, and I *may* respond not by offering grounds for *p* but by explaining how *I* came into a position to be apprised of *p*.

But since a claim of personal qualification is already implicit in a simple statement of *p*, such a statement may also be challenged in either way. ("That is a chestnut." "How do *you* know?" "I took a forestry course.") Thus, it *is*, in these cases, a matter of indifference whether the implicit or explicit form is used, although one or the other will be more appropriate in given contexts (see passage 591).

At the same time, the explicit form has special uses, which the implicit form lacks. Wittgenstein points this out when he says that even when one can replace "I know" by "it is," "one cannot replace the negation of the one by the negation of the other. With 'I don't know . . .' a new element enters our language-games" (passage 593). "I know *p*" implicitly states a fact (*p*) and explicitly states another fact, namely, a particular relation between a person and the first fact (*p*). P alone cannot be said to do this.

90. "I know" has a primitive meaning similar to and related to "I see" ("wissen," "videre"). And "I knew he was in the room, but he wasn't in the room" is like "I saw him in the room, but he wasn't there." "I know" is supposed to express a relation, not between me and the sense of a proposition (like "I believe") but between me and a fact. . . .

When *p* is explicitly stated by a person, the fact of the relation is implicit. But a different and more complex relation, the negation of the first relation, cannot be expressed implicitly with the same ease. "I don't know *p*" expressly denies either that I can offer grounds for *p* or that, if I can offer grounds for *p*, I consider the grounds compelling for belief in *p*.

Having seen that "I know *p*" conveys the relation between a person and a fact explicitly, we can ask whether there are other ways in which the same relation can be stated explicitly and, thus, whether there are other locutions with just the same use. Wittgenstein suggests two possibilities when he says that in some cases we substitute "You can rely on it; that's how it is" or "I am sure it is so" for "I know it" (passage 176). He adds, however, that one cannot *always* substitute "You can rely on it" for "I know" (passage 561) and that " 'I am sure' tells you my subjective certainty," while saying " 'I know' means that I who know it, and the person who doesn't are separated by a difference in understanding" (passage 563). In the same passage, he adds two examples and his comments about them need unpacking. He says that "if I say 'I know' in mathematics, then the justification for this is a proof," but also that "one says 'I know that he is in pain' although one can produce no convincing grounds for this." [5]

As I understand Wittgenstein's several distinctions and their applications to the mathematics example and the example, "I know that he is in pain," he is suggesting that one says "You can rely on it" or "I am sure" to forestall giving grounds or to preempt doing so, or to affirm one's authoritative understanding. One says "You can rely on it" when a demonstration, for example, by mathematical proof, is circumstantially unavailable. "You can rely on it" means "Accept it on authority rather than grounds." Although "I know" may be used in this way as well, it is likely to be a promissory note or a commitment to give grounds.

To summarize, "You can rely on it" and "I know" both affirm that the speaker is qualified to make ("stake") a claim. But "You can rely on it" annuls any move in the direction of giving grounds; it affirms qualification *tout court.* "I know" is often the opposite, a gesture toward grounds.

243. One says "I know" when one is ready to give compelling grounds. "I know" is related to a possibility of demonstrating the truth. Whether someone knows something can come to light, assuming that he is convinced of it. . . .

The same objection that is raised against "You can rely on it" as a synonym for "I know" is relevant to "I am sure" and "I am certain." Neither involves a commitment to having grounds or to giving them, although both are compatible with having and giving grounds. (They do

5. See also passages 443, 585, 586, 588.

not deny that I have grounds or imply that I do not have them.) This, I assume, is what leads Wittgenstein to say that they express a personal or subjective attitude to a fact rather than the objective relationship of being able to give grounds.[6]

The observation that "I know," unlike "I am sure," does not express subjective certainty (see passage 563) introduces further questions about the uses of "I know." In the next section, I shall discuss the fallacy that "I know p" must *either* express subjective certainty about p, *or* insure that p is true. In fact, it does neither.

Knowing: insurance and assurance

11. We just do not see how very specialized the use of "I know" is.

12. —For "I know" seems to describe a state of affairs which guarantees what is known, guarantees it as a fact. One always forgets the expression "I thought I knew."

Why does "I know" seem to "describe a state of affairs which guarantees what is known?" The problem is derived from the logic of knowing-claims. "I know p" is true only if p is true. In this respect, knowing differs from such so-called subjective attitudes as being sure, believing, being certain, thinking, etc. On discovering that p is false, I will not withdraw my claim to have believed it or have been certain of it, but I will withdraw my claim to have known it. In other words, on discovering that p is false, I will cease to believe it, cease to be certain of it, but not cease to know it; rather, I will (in this situation) be in the position of never having known it. "I only thought I knew."

It is important to distinguish the correct view that I cannot know (or have known) anything that is false from the absurd view that I cannot claim to know, or give grounds for, anything that is false. Claiming to believe differs from claiming to know in that the latter, but not the former, is a commitment to give grounds. This is part of what is meant by saying that claiming to believe is claiming something "subjective" while claiming to know is not. It follows that claiming to know is more,

6. I shall show in the last part of this chapter that the difference between knowing and believing is not merely that between an objective and a subjective claim. Wittgenstein avoids such simplification (and confusion).

rather than less, "vulnerable" than claiming to believe, for it is vulnerable in two complementary ways. First, one's grounds may not be compelling or may not be exhaustive; whether this is so is not something one can decide for oneself by fiat.[7] Second, when one's grounds are undermined, one must withdraw (as we have seen) both p and the claim to have known p. That is, one must concede that both p and "I know p" (or "I knew p") are false.

The assertion that "I know" guarantees what is known rests on a confusion between knowing and claiming to know. On the one hand, it is a logical point that knowing guarantees what is known, not because a claim to know is invulnerable but because a vulnerable and refuted claim to know is not a case of knowing but of thinking one knows. On the other hand, the *claim* "I know" does not guarantee or insure the truth of the object of the claim (the act of claiming p does not guarantee p), although it implies that the claimant believes p, is prepared to give grounds for p, etc.

Wittgenstein is, I think, making this distinction when he asks, "What is the proof that I *know* something?" and responds, "most certainly not my saying I know it" (passage 487). He observes that "it would surely be remarkable if we had to believe the reliable person who says 'I can't be wrong'" (passage 22). Indeed, "it might surely happen that whenever I said 'I know' it turned out to be wrong" (passage 580). He adds the observation that Moore makes this mistake, that Moore thinks that "know" is analogous to "surmise" or "believe," insofar as "I know" cannot be a mistake, insofar as one can infer "from such an utterance to the truth of the assertion" (passage 21). Thus, "I know," said sincerely, insures *not* the truth of the assertion but only that the speaker *thinks* he knows.[8]

In these passages Wittgenstein is pointing to two fallacies. The first is the view that the utterance "I know" is like "I believe" or "I think" or "I surmise" in that, said in appropriate circumstances and without deceit (including self-deceit), it is "self-insuring" and *cannot* be a mistake.

---

7. This point is discussed in chapter three.
8. Passage 21, as I read it, is a reductio ad absurdum of the suggested assimilation of "I know" to "I believe."

(Note for comparison that "I believe *p*" *is* self-insuring, but only where there is no self-deception. I *may* concede "I only thought I believed *p*" if I have deceived myself and discover beliefs that I hold but that are incompatible with *p*.)

The second fallacy is that because the truth of *p* follows from the fact that I know *p,* the truth of *p* follows from the fact of my claiming to know *p.* The second fallacy appears plausible because, again barring deceit, I will not claim to know unless *it seems to me* I also know; knowing *seems* a condition of my nondeceitful behavior of claiming to know. But this is again to forget the possibility of a mistake. Thinking that I know, rather than knowing, is to be identified with my nondeceitful behavior of claiming to know.

13. ... [I]t is not as though the proposition "It is so" could be inferred from someone else's utterance: "I know it is so." Nor from the utterance together with its not being a lie.—But can't I infer "It is so" from my own utterance "I know etc."? Yes; and also "There is a hand there" follows from the proposition "He knows that there's a hand there." But from the utterance "I know..." it does not follow that he does know it.

Note that passage 13 is muddled. Wittgenstein notwithstanding, I *cannot* infer "It is so" from my own utterance "I know etc." any more than I can infer from my utterance that the utterance is not a mistake. I can infer "It is so" only from the truth of my utterance. Thus, it is correct to say that I can infer that there is a hand there from the proposition, taken as *true,* that "he knows that there's a hand there," but I cannot infer it from his or anyone else's utterance.

WITTGENSTEIN'S CRITIQUE OF MOORE

Introduction In "Proof of the External World," [9] as elsewhere, G. E. Moore claims to refute both skepticism and idealism based on skepticism by resorting to such so-called indubitable propositions as "I know that this is my hand." Such propositions, Moore claims, are incompatible with skeptical idealism, the view that I must and cannot justify references to a real world of external objects. *On Certainty* is, in large part,

9. Contained in G. E. Moore's *Philosophical Papers* (New York: Collier Books, 1962; originally published in London: George Allen and Unwin, 1939).

Wittgenstein's examination of Moore's arguments. I shall not be concerned with the adequacy (as a representation of Moore) of Wittgenstein's reconstruction of the argument, but only with the nature and merits of Wittgenstein's discussion of it.[10]

The sort of skeptical position that Moore is seeking to refute is a familiar and general one. It says that we cannot know about the existence even of everyday physical objects, objects such as our own hands or the trees before us, for in each case of claiming to know (and therefore in every case) it is possible that we may be deluded, imagining things, etc. The fact that we can give grounds for *thinking* that we are not deluded, not imagining things, etc., counts not at all toward establishing conclusively that we are not deluded, etc., for we may be deluded about those very matters which we offer as grounds.

Moore's strategy in responding is to distinguish the claim that I cannot prove that I have not been deluded or dreaming from the claim that I cannot prove that there are external objects. He concedes the first point and denies the second. He claims that one can prove that there are physical objects by taking a premise of which one is certain and deriving from it a conclusion about the existence of an external object:

Here is one proof. I can say: "I held up two hands above this desk not very long ago; therefore two hands existed not very long ago; therefore at least two external objects have existed at some time in the past, Q.E.D." This is a perfectly good proof, provided I *know* what is asserted in the premise. But I *do* know that I held up two hands above this desk not very long ago. As a matter of fact, in this case you all know it too. There's no doubt whatever that I did. Therefore I have given a perfectly conclusive proof that external objects have existed in the past.[11]

But *how* do I know the premise? (The skeptic, of course, denies that I know the premise.) Moore says that he has conclusive reasons for the premise, and for other premises like "I am not dreaming," but he admits

10. It can be argued, persuasively I think, that Moore's conclusions about the relation of convictions to justification are much closer to Wittgenstein's views than will be apparent from the rest of my discussion. In spirit, Wittgenstein seems to me much closer to Moore's views about these matters than, say, to skepticism in any form. But see note 19, below.

11. Moore, op. cit., p. 146.

that having conclusive reasons is a very different thing from being able to give a proof of the premise.

In order to [prove the premise], I should need to prove for one thing, as Descartes pointed out, that I am not dreaming. But how can I prove that I am not? I have, no doubt, conclusive reasons for asserting that I am not now dreaming; I have conclusive evidence that I am awake: but that is a very different thing from being able to prove it. I could not tell you what all my evidence is; and I should require to do this at least, in order to give you a proof.[12]

Such premises, then, as "I know that this is a tree" or "I know that that is my hand" are claims for which I have conclusive evidence (or reasons) but which I cannot prove. The skeptic errs, according to Moore, in saying that I am entitled to claim knowledge only if I can offer a proof and in supposing that there is no such thing as conclusive evidence in the absence of a proof.

The basic theme of Wittgenstein's response to Moore is:

521. Moore's mistake lies in this—countering the assertion that one cannot know that, by saying "I do know it."

But why is it wrong to counter the assertion in this way? If it *is* wrong, how (if at all) can skeptical idealism be countered?

Wittgenstein and Moore: agreement and disagreement Before taking up these questions, I want to emphasize ways in which Moore and Wittgenstein agree, points of agreement which Wittgenstein recognizes as such. This is explicit in the following passages.

397. Haven't I gone wrong and isn't Moore perfectly right? Haven't I made the elementary mistake of confusing one's thoughts with one's knowledge? Of course I do not think to myself "The earth already existed for some time before my birth," but do I *know* it any the less? Don't I show that I know it by always drawing the consequences?
398. And don't I know that there is no stairway in this house going six floors deep into the earth, even though I have never thought about it?
424. ... But what about this: "If I were to tell someone that that was a tree, that wouldn't be just surmise." Isn't this what Moore was trying to say?

12. Ibid., p. 148.

And *if* Moore was trying to say this, he was correct. That this is my hand, or that that is a tree, is not a surmise on the basis of particular evidence. Further, while Moore says that I have evidence (conclusive evidence, he says) for the conviction that I am awake, he is concerned to stress that I do not need to seek particular evidence for it. Without particular evidence, my being awake is as certain as such things can be. These conclusions are shared by Moore and Wittgenstein. Moreover, they agree that knowing, e.g., that I have five toes on my right foot, may be attributed to me even when it would be inapposite' and misleading for me to say that I know this.

If there is so much agreement, what is the focus of criticism? One possible criticism is that Moore confuses what can be said about *knowing* with what can be said about *claiming* to know, or at least that he does this at *some* points and not at others. This, however, cannot be Wittgenstein's point, for he makes clear (see passage 397 above) that he rejects Moore's premise in his "proof" *not* as the premise that he may appropriately claim to know but simply as the premise that he knows.[13] Accordingly, Wittgenstein makes clear at several points that he rejects "I know I am in pain" and "I know the earth has existed for many years" as admissible premises and not simply as inappropriate utterances; he says that it is not the case that Moore *knows* these things. In passage 91, for example, he examines Moore's claim that he knows that the earth existed, etc.; he concedes that the earth has existed all that time and that Moore is convinced of it, but he insists that Moore doesn't *know*

13. Of course, in the special context of offering a proof, it is arguable that it *is* appropriate to *claim* that he knows, for example, that that is his hand. And in this special context, no one will suppose that the claim presupposes special empirical grounds for doubt and assertion. This claim is not unjustified and presumptuous. Compare the following references (in *On Certainty*) to philosophical contexts.

467. I am sitting with a philosopher in the garden; he says again and again "I know that that's a tree," pointing to a tree that is near us. Someone else arrives and hears this, and I tell him: "This fellow isn't insane. We are only doing philosophy."

350. "I know that that's a tree" is something a philosopher might say to demonstrate to himself or to someone else that he *knows* something that is not a mathematical or logical truth. (. . . Here I have already sketched a background, a surrounding, for this remark, that is to say, given it a context.) . . .

if he does not have "the right *ground* for his conviction." He says, in passage 151, "Moore does not *know* what he asserts he knows, but it stands fast for him, as also for me; regarding it as absolutely solid is part of our *method* of doubt and enquiry." [14]

We must keep in mind a difference between the stairway example and the pain and earth examples, since Wittgenstein insists that the first example alone is a genuine case of knowing. The difference becomes clear if we recognize that one has grounds for one's conviction that there is no stairway, etc., however otiose it may be to investigate. Similarly, "I know where you touched my arm" is proper because it has grounds, while " 'I know where I am feeling pain' . . . is as wrong as 'I know that I am in pain' " (passage 41). Wittgenstein concludes that, as a general matter, "whether I *know* something depends on whether the evidence backs me up or contradicts me" (passage 504). When there is no possibility of evidence backing me up or contradicting me, the matter cannot be something that I know.

The pain and earth examples are both propositions for which one does not claim to have evidence and with regard to which a request for grounds is a sign of misunderstanding. Neither is the sort of matter which needs or *can* have justification, and therefore both are inapposite objects of "I know. . . ." The criticism is *not* merely that such claims to know would not be *made* on the basis of evidence (for "I know where you touched my arm," which is in order, is not made on the basis of evidence either). The criticism is rather that the request for grounds or evidence is inapplicable. My claim about where you touched my arm, even if not made on the basis of evidence, can be corroborated by the testimony of others since the touching is a public event. "The earth existed, etc." and "I am in pain" are, in all contexts, inapposite subjects of corroboration.

There are important differences between the pain example and the earth example. The first refers to a personal experience. I give direct expression of pain by saying "I am in pain." My utterance is both expression and self-description. I alone am in a position to express my pains; others can describe me as being in pain on the basis of my own expression of

14. See also passages 111, 136.

pain or other evidence, but not by having my pain. "I know I am in pain" is wrong but "I know he is in pain" has use. Each of us uses "I am in pain" to express *his own* personal pain experiences. In contrast, each of us uses "The earth existed, etc." (if we use it at all) to state what is shared.

389. Moore wanted to give an example to shew [*sic*] that one really can *know* propositions about physical objects.—If there were a dispute whether one could have a pain in such and such a part of the body, then someone who just then has a pain in that spot might say: "I assure you, I have a pain there now." But it would sound odd if Moore has said: "I assure you, I know that that's a tree." A personal experience simply has no interest for us here.

One is in a position, uniquely, to say "I am in pain"; a personal claim is appropriate but not a personal claim of knowledge (a personal claim to have grounds). But one is not in a position to make *any* personal claim with regard to "The earth existed, etc." Moore assimilates the two examples because he takes "I am in pain" to be exemplary of both (1) a personal claim and (2) something indubitable. He then assumes that "I know the earth existed" is similarly a personal claim and indubitable.

Wittgenstein on Moore and skepticism   I argued above that it would be wrong to interpret Wittgenstein's criticism of such claims by Moore as "I know the earth existed, etc." or "I know there are physical objects" in either of two ways. The first is the criticism that, although one *does* know these things, one cannot say that one knows. The second is the criticism that one does not know these things because they are immediate and indubitable. We need a third interpretation which explains both the distinctive character of such propositions as "There are physical objects" and "The earth existed, etc." and their inappropriateness as objects of knowledge claims.

Wittgenstein's strategy is to show that it is misleading to say either that we do or can know such matters, or that we do not and cannot know them. They are neither justified nor unjustified but simply embedded as certainties in our practices, i.e., our actions and understanding.[15]

15. I discuss this topic in chapter one.

Wittgenstein concludes that "the language-game is . . . not based on grounds. It is not reasonable (or unreasonable). It is there—like our life" (passage 559). "The end is . . . an ungrounded way of acting" (passage 110).

A genuine case of knowing is a matter of general *and* special qualification. "I know . . ." means "I have this special qualification" (which includes being qualified to give grounds); it is always conceivable that the claimant might not be so qualified. It makes sense to say of me that I know *p*, or am specially qualified, only if it would also make sense to say that I do not know *p*, am not specially qualified. Questions about knowing or special qualifications can only arise among those who are already *generally* qualified to engage in the relevant practice. Questions about general qualification will ordinarily not arise. This is simply to say (as I argued in chapter one) that questions about whether I speak English will not arise in the course of my lectures and questions about my ability to read will not arise at an academic conference (except facetiously). Moore's putative claims to know are, distinctively, all claims about general and not special qualification: "the truths which Moore says he knows are such as, roughly speaking, all of us know, if he knows them" (passage 100). As we have seen, where the matter is in principle one of general qualification, "I know, etc." is a logical proposition in which "the 'I' cannot be important. . . . 'The expression "I do not know" makes no sense in this case.' And of course it follows from this that 'I *know*' makes no sense either" (passage 58).[16]

Let us say that I claim to know a fact in Nepalese history. In doing so, I imply that I am specially qualified and that I can give grounds for my claim. There is ordinarily no question of my being qualified to speak English or read or discuss general history. Claims like "I know how to read" or "I know that this is my hand" have a use only when they can be construed as claims of special qualification, and such cases are unusual. One example is a claim made by a child to display linguistic facility. When not all children know how to use "physical object," a child who says "I know that this is a physical object" claims to be specially qualified.[17]

---

16. See also passages 32, 84, 101, 116, 157.
17. Note that whenever it makes sense to question qualifications, it also makes

We have already seen that "I know p" expresses a relationship between a speaker and a fact that can be found out (see passage 90), the relationship of being able to give grounds that the speaker regards (and expects others will regard) as compelling. In those rare contexts where it means anything at all, "I know there are physical objects" means "I can show that there are things which persons generally call 'physical objects.'" It affirms that the speaker is qualified to play the language-game (in contrast to those who are not qualified), to say what physical objects are, etc. In this sense, it affirms that the speaker is "normal" and has use when normality is in question.

441. In a court of law the mere assurance "I know..." on the part of a witness would convince no one. It must be shown that he was in a position to know.

Even the assurance "I know that that's a hand," said while someone looked at his own hand, would not be credible unless we knew the circumstances in which it was said. And if we do know them, it seems to be an assurance that the person speaking is normal in this respect.

We can now frame the following criticism of Moore. In each of his examples he claims not a special but a general qualification and that cannot be expressed by "I know...." Wittgenstein concludes that one slips into using "know" mistakenly for matters "of such a kind that it is difficult to imagine why anyone should believe the contrary," and that Moore characteristically does so (passage 93) because one does "not see how specialized the use of 'I know' is" (passage 11).[18] The use of "I know" is specialized in the sense that one may easily slip from a clear move in a knowing-game to a move that is not at all clear. "I know how long this house has been here" is an intelligible move in a readily constructed conversation. "I know how long this mountain has been here" is an intelligible move in a game in which participants are presumed to

---

sense to claim to know. Thus, "I know the earth existed, etc." may be (in particular circumstances) a way of saying "I know how to do history," and "I know that $2 \times 2 = 4$" may be a way of saying "I know how to multiply." We saw earlier that it may be appropriate to meet a challenge to "I know that p" either by giving grounds for p or by showing how I came to be in a position to give grounds for p. The cases here are of the latter kind.

18. See also passages 18, 85.

have specialized geological knowledge and are not like children who think that mountains have always been here. We can easily imagine persons among whom the claim is not intelligible, but we cannot imagine it unintelligible among persons with whom we share a world-picture. But "I know that the earth existed two hundred years ago" is intelligible as a move in a knowing-game only if this issue is alive and debatable, and if there is shared recognition of what counts as *special* qualification to make such a claim and give grounds. Remember also that these remarks are not about the contextual appropriateness of *claims* to know but about knowing itself: A is less and less likely to be thought of as knowing *p* (and less and less likely to regard himself as knowing *p*) to the extent that *p* is such that one cannot imagine how "anyone should believe the contrary" (see passage 93).

It follows that the distinctive use of "I know" to refute skepticism and to prove what is most certainly beyond doubt and beyond questioning is misconceived.

407. For when Moore says "I know that that's ..." I want to reply "you don't *know* anything"—and yet I would not say that to anyone who was speaking without philosophical intention. That is, I feel (rightly?) that these two mean to say something different.

The "philosophical intention" is the intention to refute skepticism. Wittgenstein's own intention is to show that the matters raised by skeptics (and by Moore) are not the sorts of things for which grounds can be produced or the sorts of things for which grounds are needed.

"I know that that is my hand" "I know that that is my hand" is the premise of Moore's proof of the external world. The "hand" example is different in some respects from both the pain and the earth examples. Unlike "I am in pain," "This is my hand" does not ordinarily convey information about myself, information to which I have privileged access. Unlike "The earth existed, etc." the statement is about (a part of) myself, a statement each person can make about him/herself. By discussing and grouping together some of Wittgenstein's remarks about this one example, we can review the critique of Moore. In comparing this example with others, we see also that there is an indefinite array of kinds

of nonevidentiary propositions, all of which are not proper objects of "I know...," but for special and different reasons in each case.

There are easily imagined but unusual situations in which "I know that that is my hand" is a perfectly understandable claim. For example, if someone assures me that he has two hands when it is uncertain whether they have been amputated, I will believe his claim insofar as I think "it is possible for him to make sure" (passage 23) and insofar as I think he is trustworthy. The intelligibility of the knowing claim depends on the intelligibility of the question "How do you know?"; the claim is appropriate when and only when one can "add how one knows" (passage 40).

Ordinarily of course one cannot "add how one knows" or indicate how anyone could have grounds for doubt (passages 445, 372). Moore, to be sure, is not imagining special contexts but says that in ordinary contexts I know that this is my hand. It is misleading to offer this as a special (i.e., personal) qualification, and "I know" implies special qualification.

32. It's not a matter of *Moore's* knowing that there's a hand there, but rather we should not understand him if he were to say "Of course I may be wrong about this." We should ask "What is it like to make such a mistake as that?" —e.g. what's it like to discover that it was a mistake?

This is a point against the skeptic insofar as the skeptic is claiming that we know what it would be like to make a mistake in this and comparable cases.[19]

According to Wittgenstein, the claim Moore is trying to make is a claim of general qualification: "I am generally qualified to engage in this practice; I know, for example, how to use the word 'hand.'" And Moore is also making a general claim about the practice: "Such a claim cannot be doubted without doubting one's capacity to make any judgments whatever."

19. I am assuming here that the skeptic claims that in every situation it is either the case that "I know..." or that I may be making a mistake and that apparent cases of the first kind are really cases of the second and are, therefore, not proper cases of knowing. This may not be the skeptic's point at all, however. His point may involve no reference to the possibility of mistake or of being wrong. He may simply deny that apparent cases of knowing are such that I can give grounds or know what grounds are apposite; in this case, his point is the same as Wittgenstein's.

369. If I wanted to doubt whether this was my hand, how could I avoid doubting whether the word "hand" has any meaning? So that is something I seem to *know* after all.[20]

But the lingering mistake in saying that it is something I know is that there is no special qualification, no answer to *how* I know. Notwithstanding that I have no doubt that this is my hand, notwithstanding that this conviction is "a foundation for all my action," this state of conviction is "wrongly expressed by the words 'I know'" (passage 414). Unlike Moore, Wittgenstein is able to use this distinction between knowing (which is not apposite) and acting "with a certainty that knows no doubt" (which *is* apposite) to respond to the challenge posed by skepticism (passage 360).[21] Wittgenstein's characteristic response to the skeptic, here as elsewhere, is that, however I exercise my imagination, I cannot act in accord with the skeptic's hypotheses nor can I imagine my general qualifications to be special qualifications in need of grounding. Skepticism has no consequences for how I proceed in action, and if "I shall *act* with a certainty that knows no doubt," I (simply) have no doubt.

KNOWING AND BELIEVING

This discussion of the uses of "I know" and of skepticism has special implications for questions about the relationship of knowledge and belief. One form of skepticism is the recommendation that every knowledge claim be demoted to a belief claim: when I say "I know . . ." I should more properly say "I believe I know. . . ." The latter is all one is entitled to say. Wittgenstein asks us to suppose that we were forbidden to say "I know" and permitted to say only "I believe I know" (passage 366), and responds that nothing would be gained and something lost by this modification. He would criticize the skeptical suggestion on these grounds: it is not more correct but more misleading to say that we only "believe" what we claim to know. "I believe" has its own special uses,

20. See also passage 268.
21. See also passages 412, 413.

as we shall see below, and they are not to be confused with the uses of "I know."

In order to examine more closely these uses and Wittgenstein's attempts to distinguish knowing from believing, I shall look first at general remarks about the logic of knowing-claims and believing-claims and then at the relevance of these remarks to the critique of Moore.

The difference between knowing-claims and believing-claims is not a difference in *degree* of certainty and commitment; belief is not simply a weaker or more attenuated commitment to a proposition than knowing. To be sure, we sometimes say "I believe . . ." when we hold *p* tentatively. But we also say "I believe *p*" when we hold *p* very strongly indeed but cannot give reasons, or (more specifically) cannot commit ourselves to giving grounds for *p* which we expect others to recognize and accept as grounds.

The difference is, secondly, not a difference between two different attitudes or mental states.

42. . . . It would . . . be *possible* to speak of a mental state of conviction, and that may be the same whether it is knowledge or false belief. To think that different states must correspond to the words "believe" and "know" would be as if one believes that different people had to correspond to the word "I" and the name "Ludwig," because the concepts are different.

Rather, the difference between claims of knowledge and claims of belief is that only knowledge claims commit the speaker to give reasons. When one claims to know, one holds oneself out as being capable of saying how one knows; when one claims to believe, one does not necessarily hold oneself out as capable of saying why one believes (passage 550). We judge whether someone is in a position to know but not whether someone is in a position to believe (passage 556). " 'I know it' I say to someone else and here there is a justification. But there is none for my belief" (passage 175).[22]

Note also that the difference between knowledge-claims and belief-claims does not explain the difference between knowledge and belief. Although "I believe *p*" does not commit me to being able to give reasons

22. See also passages 179, 180, 483, 484, 485, 489.

for p, it does not preempt the possibility of giving reasons. But even if I do give reasons and even if I claim to know p rather than to believe p, my relationship to p will be one of belief and not one of knowledge *if p turns out to be false*.[23] Thus, the difference between knowledge-*claims* and belief-*claims* is that only the first involves a commitment to give reasons; the difference between knowledge and belief depends on whether what is claimed turns out to be true and not on the strength of conviction or on the readiness to give grounds.

One further point about knowledge and belief (but not about knowledge- and belief-claims) is that believing p is a condition of knowing p. However misleading it is to *claim* to believe p when one is prepared to claim to know p, it is logically the case that

177. What I know, I believe.

Given the relationship of knowledge-claims and belief-claims just outlined, we can extend some of our earlier discoveries about knowing-claims to belief-claims. For example, whenever "I know p" is out of order because p is a methodological proposition, "I believe p" (e.g., "I believe there are physical objects") will be out of order for the same reasons. Although "I believe p" does not imply a commitment to give reasons, it does presuppose a readiness to treat p as optional, to submit p for testing and examination.

Some of the same difficulties affect "I believe p" where p is not a methodological proposition, but a proposition held fast in the particular context; "I believe that this is my hand" makes sense in special, but not in ordinary contexts. Thus, my conviction that this is my hand, that my name is T. M., or that the earth existed, etc., is not *just* a belief. I can speak of believing where I can also intelligibly speak of not believing, but these matters are such that, in the relevant contexts, my sureness of them is a condition of my making any judgments at all.

486. "Do you know or do you only believe that your name is L. W.?" Is that a meaningful question?

Do you know or do you only believe that what you are writing down now

---

23. This is what Wittgenstein seems to be saying in passage 42.

are German words? Do you only believe that "believe" has *this* meaning? *What* meaning? [24]

(Throughout this section, "belief" is used in the sense of "surmise." We saw above that there is another sense in which the convictions that are the bases of my practices are things I can be said to believe.)

It is important that my being certain and not merely believing (e.g., about my name) is compatible with my being able to see experiences as recalcitrant, recalcitrant even to convictions that in present and expected contexts cannot be doubted without abandoning all judgment. I can imagine recalcitrant experiences that lead me to change, even radically, my conception of the context. I may anticipate that no future experience will seem to impeach my certainty, but this does not insure that there will be no such experiences. One cannot have special qualifications or grounds for *knowing* that such experiences will not happen. [25]

24. See also passages 308, 490, 506, 507.
25. See passages 356, 364, 365.

Five

On Unreasonable and Impossible Doubt

Let us look more closely at the distinction between (1) empirical propositions held fast as "rules for judging" and (2) methodological propositions. I argued in chapter four, in agreement with Wittgenstein, that propositions of type (1) can be the objects of knowing-claims only when they are not held fast. An example is "My name is T. M." in a context in which there is reason to question my name. By contrast, a methodological proposition, like "There are physical objects," is never intelligible as the object of a knowledge-claim. Another point is that empirical propositions name things that one knows even when they are held fast: I know that my name is T. M. even when there is no occasion to question or doubt it, or to say it. Methodological propositions do not name things that I know.

673. Is it not difficult to distinguish between the cases in which I cannot and those in which I can *hardly* be mistaken? Is it always clear to which kind a case belongs? I believe not.
454. There are cases where doubt is unreasonable, but others where it seems logically impossible. And there seems to be no clear boundary between them.

A methodological proposition is a proposition about which I *cannot* be mistaken, one where doubt is logically impossible. Accordingly, it seems to me that these passages refer to the distinction between (1) and (2).

In this chapter I shall explore the distinction and discuss its importance. The notion of a methodological proposition is like the notion of a proposition known a priori, a proposition which invariably specifies a condition for the possibility of knowing.[1]

MAKING A MISTAKE AND BEING MISTAKEN

The claim that there is an intelligible distinction between (1) and (2) is challengeable. In particular, it can be argued that for a particular p, it cannot be demonstrated that p is a methodological proposition rather than a proposition held fast in some or many contexts. The reason is that it is not possible to survey all possible contexts to demonstrate that there is no context in which p is dubitable.

The argument proceeds as follows. With regard to some p's, one can readily think of circumstances in which p is dubitable; for example, "I have two hands" may be in question after a mutilating accident. With regard to other p's, p will be dubitable only in quite extraordinary circumstances; an example is "I have never been on the planet Mars." But no p is such that one can think of all circumstances in which p might be relevant. If this is so, one can never be in a position to claim that there will be *no* circumstances in which p is dubitable. P may simply be such that the speaker cannot readily describe a context of dubitability. And not only this: I (as speaker) am not even entitled to claim with certainty that the *present* circumstances are not (for reasons which I fail to realize) the very ones in which p ought to be doubted.

Thus, although the claim that I can hardly be mistaken is correct for some p's, it is never correct that I cannot be mistaken. Or, the claim is often correct that doubt about p is unreasonable, but never that it is logically impossible. In each case, the latter claim requires me to have canvassed all possible circumstances and to have excluded *any* possibility that the present circumstances (the context in which the claim is made) are ones in which doubting p is, after all, reasonable.[2]

1. See my paper, "Wittgenstein and Synthetic A Priori Propositions," *Philosophy,* vol. 49 (1974), pp. 429–434.
2. One way of talking about matters where doubt is logically impossible is to say that they are true in every possible world. By contrast, matters where doubt is unreasonable may be matters held fast in the actual world but false in imaginable possible worlds. I do not pursue this way of making the distinction in this chapter, but it seems compatible with several distinctions which I *do* make.

This is a strong argument. It seems obvious that we cannot canvass all possible circumstances and claim, with regard to *p*, that it would have to be held fast in all possible ones. I shall try to show that we do not need to do this to defend the original distinction. We need a different criterion for methodological propositions, and in the rest of this chapter, particularly in the section "Impossible Doubt," I shall try to indicate what such a criterion might be.[3]

Wittgenstein gives little help with this problem. He is concerned generally to distinguish cases where doubt is *un*reasonable from cases where doubt *is* reasonable and not from cases where doubt is logically impossible. Typically (as in the following passage), he seems to suggest that once it is shown that doubt about *p* is unreasonable, further discussion of *p* is otiose.

120. But if anyone were to doubt it, how would his doubt come out in practice? And couldn't we peacefully leave him to doubt it, since it makes no difference at all?

Without offering criteria yet, we can make clearer the distinction between (1) reasonable doubt, (2) unreasonable doubt, and (3) logically impossible doubt, by looking at a parallel distinction between (1) making a mistake, (2) being mistaken (or being wrong) but not *making* a mistake, and (3) cases in which mistake is logically impossible. A case in which I can have a reasonable doubt about *p* is a case in which I can be making a mistake (e.g., in which *p* is a hypothesis, a guess, etc.). A doubt can be fitted with those things which are not doubted and into "correct" procedures for testing beliefs. We have already seen that an error which cannot be fitted into such procedures is to be described not as an instance of making a mistake but, perhaps by default, as a symptom of mental disturbance (passage 71). Wittgenstein offers the example of

3. Kant's notion of synthetic a priori propositions has this in common with what I call "methodological propositions": Both are defined as propositions held fast not in some contexts of experience but in experience generally. Further, they are in some sense necessarily true of experience generally. I examine in this chapter whether it makes sense to say that any propositions have this character. The question whether any experience can ever be said to disconfirm a synthetic a priori judgment is controversial in the interpretation of Kant. I try to confront the problem indirectly in this chapter. See also note 1 above.

the man who is wrong about his own address (passage 71) or about the fact that he has just had lunch. "If I say to someone 'I have just eaten' he may believe that I am lying or have momentarily lost my wits but he won't believe that I am making a mistake" (passage 659). At the same time, there are ready ways of explaining such an error through temporary disorientation and disturbance: "I might have dropped off immediately after the meal without knowing it and have slept for an hour" (passage 659) or "I might have imagined [having spent the morning with a friend] to myself in a dreamy way" (passage 648).[4]

The paranoiac or the man who claims to have the wrong address is not making a mistake but *is* mistaken, and so are the persons in passages 648 and 659. (Clearly these matters are not exhausted by the distinction between mistake and mental disturbance as drawn in chapter two.) If I have fallen asleep and dreamt the most recent "year" of my life, I am not (just) making a mistake (my problem is greater than that) but I *am* mistaken about many things. Thus, for a great array of cases, "I cannot be *making* a mistake" is compatible with "(It is logically possible that) I can be wrong and I can be mistaken." I can, as Wittgenstein does in passages 648 and 659, describe just those circumstances in which I would be wrong. My capacity to offer such an imaginative account does not make doubt reasonable; doubt is unreasonable unless experience offers grounds for thinking such a story is true.

How can we determine whether there are matters in class (3), about which I cannot be mistaken? We have looked at and rejected one strategy, that of canvassing possible circumstances seriatim and asking whether p is dubitable in each case. Other strategies suggest themselves. I can ask whether some p's are such that they are not affected by the hypothesis that I have "dreamed the whole thing," or momentarily lost my wits. Another strategic question is whether I can tell a story in which p turns out to be false. Are there matters about which I cannot tell such a story? Finally, a third question is whether some p's are such that the very idea of having grounds or finding corroborating experiences (or the opposite, disconfirming experiences) is incompatible with them.

I shall try to show that Wittgenstein's own examples suggest these

4. See also passages 72, 73, 74; see discussion of mental disturbance, chapter two.

putative criteria. But first, I shall look more closely at the heterogeneous matters about which I can *hardly* be mistaken, about which doubt is unreasonable. Then I shall examine the criteria for cases in which doubt is logically impossible and suggest why, as Wittgenstein says (passage 673), "it is not always clear to which kind a case belongs."

UNREASONABLE DOUBT

17. Suppose now I say "I'm incapable of being wrong about this: that is a book" while I point to an object. What would a mistake here be like? And have I any *clear* idea of it?
25. One may be wrong even about "there being a hand here." Only in particular circumstances is it impossible.—"Even in a calculation one can be wrong—only in certain circumstances one can't."

Of course, passages 648 and 659 point to "clear ideas" about what a mistake in these cases *would* be like, a slip of the tongue or perhaps a temporary delusion. But the core of such examples is complete but misplaced confidence: the mistake can only be entertained by a hearer or by speaker dissociated from the circumstances of his utterance. Thus, I (as speaker in the examples) can invest no confidence in the possibility that this is not a book, that this is not my hand. I am as certain as I can be and would reject putative counterevidence out of hand. An X ray showing my hand to be made of plastic and metal would be inexplicable, a fraud.

645. I can't be making a mistake,—but some day, rightly or wrongly, I may think I realize that I was not competent to judge.[5]

Even when I have no clear idea of how I can possibly be wrong (about the book, my hand, my name), I can of course tell a story in which I discover the book is a radio, or my hand passes through the "book" like vapor, or the bizarre X ray of my hand is produced. Such stories do not show *either* that my certainty is misplaced *or* that such experiences would (if they occurred) force me to give up my certainty and admit that I was wrong. Rather, in such situations "evidence is facing evidence, and it

5. See also passages 437, 660, 667.

must be *decided* which is to give way." It is necessary to distinguish these situations from ones in which certainty *is* misplaced, to distinguish among different "ways in which something 'turns out wrong' " (passage 641). The point of devising such stories is that we can think of *having to reject* such imaginable counterevidence to retain our certainty. The point is also that in the face of many bizarre and unexpected (counterevidentiary) experiences it may well be unreasonable to continue to judge as one has been judging or even to trust one's ways of judging at all.

617. Certain events would put me into a position in which I could not go on with the old language-game any further. In which I was torn away from the *sureness* of the game.

Indeed, doesn't it seem obvious that the possibility of a language-game is conditioned by certain facts?

The list of examples of which all this can be said is long and diverse, but each is an example of something appropriately taken for granted in a context.[6] In other words, when I say "I cannot be making a mistake" I mean that I cannot be mistaken except in ways that I have no way of detecting, controlling, or precluding. Is there a paradox in the use of "I can't be wrong" and "I can't be mistaken," since these propositions may be used properly even in cases when the speaker does indeed turn out to be wrong? Wittgenstein takes the example of someone who says appropriately, "I can't be mistaken about my name" and yet turns out to be mistaken after all. He asks whether this makes "I can't be mistaken . . ." nonsense, whether it would be better to say "I can hardly be mistaken." But "I can hardly be mistaken" has a different use and does not do the job required (passages 596, 633). He concludes that

638. "I can't be making a mistake" is an ordinary sentence, which serves to give the certainty-value of a statement. And only in its everyday use is it justified.[7]

Wittgenstein's conclusion (in 638) looks paradoxical. He seems to endorse my saying "I can't be making a mistake," "I can't be mistaken," or "I can't be wrong" when it is *really* the case that I can hardly be mistaken,

6. Other examples are in passages 32, 157, 594, 634, 636, 675.
7. See also passages 595, 598, 643.

i.e., that certain kinds of failure, those kinds which I can detect and eliminate by fitting my procedure to what I already "know aright," are excluded. I cannot *say* in these situations "I can hardly be mistaken" because that "means something else" (passage 633), something weaker than I intend. (Note again the difference between what is the case and what can be claimed to be the case. As there are cases in which I know *p* but cannot, without misleading or puzzling my hearers, *say* that I know, so too there are cases in which I can hardly be mistaken but in which I cannot say, "I can hardly be mistaken.") What I say is "I cannot be making a mistake," and this is justified "only in its everyday use" (passage 638). The conclusion is not in fact paradoxical, for the residual sources of mistakes are those against which the speaker cannot guard and which are excluded from consideration except in specially appropriate circumstances.

445. But if I say "I have two hands," what can I add to indicate reliability? At the most that the circumstances are the ordinary ones.
446. But why *am* I so certain that this is my hand? Doesn't the whole language-game rest on this kind of certainty?
  Or: isn't this "certainty" already presupposed in the language-game? Namely by virtue of the fact that one is not playing the game, or is playing it wrong, if one does not recognize objects with certainty.[8]

Another way of making my argument is to say that "I cannot be mistaken in trusting my eyes" has two uses. In ordinary use it means (1) in *this* case I have and impute no grounds for thinking that my eyes are not reliable.[9] This presumption (i.e., that the situation is not relevantly unusual) is rebuttable. But the claim has philosophical (logical, in Wittgen-

---

8. See also passage 125.
9. This is not to deny that there are general visual disabilities like color blindness. The color-blind person, aware of the disability, will give up judging the affected colors altogether. One denies, as noted, the general possibility of such a disability in saying "I can hardly be mistaken." One may be wrong in a general denial of color blindness but not in a general denial of the hypothesis that all visual experience is hallucinatory. The former denial can be fitted into other experiences (e.g., what others say) and judged accordingly; the latter cannot. I can come to realize on the basis of grounds that I am color-blind but not that all my visual experiences are hallucinations.

stein's sense[10]) significance as well. It means that, given the situation described in (1), I *must* trust my eyes when I judge; it means (2) that if I do not trust my eyes in general, there is much else that I cannot do, practices of judging that I must give up.

The cases we have so far canvassed of unreasonable doubt are cases of cognitive failure or deficiency. They involve the relation of persons to their cognitive faculties. There are other cases of unreasonable doubt that have to do *not* with cognition's being (or not being) as one supposes it to be but with the world's (and one's experiences in the world) being (or not being) as one supposes it to be. One may imagine that one has been transported to the moon and back by unknown means, in sleep, but this possibility does not give grounds for reasonable doubt or for speaking of a possible mistake. "My not having been on the moon is as sure a thing for me as any grounds I could give for it" (passage 111). To speak of a possible mistake here is "to play the game wrong" (passage 662).[11] We see the same general point as above: being wrong or being mistaken is so unlikely and undeterminable as to be discounted. It is both unlikely and incompatible with trusting my judgment. "I cannot be making a mistake" emphasizes that a mistake here is "unheard-of" (but not logically impossible.) Science fiction posits extraordinary and untestable hypotheses that, if realized and experienced, would compel us to alter our conception of how things are. Considering such stories does not, as Wittgenstein emphasizes, "give me any right to speak of a possible mistake."

Before looking at cases of impossible doubt, let us summarize some points about unreasonable doubt.

1. The question "Can you be mistaken (about not having been on the moon, about your name, about *this* being your hand)?" is most likely to be a question about circumstances, carrying the suggestion that the circumstances may be relevantly extraordinary. The suggestion will have to be backed by evidence that shows why, e.g., a lapse of consciousness or a mistake about my name is to be suspected and how it can be fitted with

10. See chapter two.
11. See also passages 93, 218, 222, 661.

other matters about which I am not wrong. Such evidence will change my conception of the context and, therefore, of the possibility of being mistaken. Even if I know that I am prone to unwitting lapses of consciousness, I can qualify my judgments to accommodate this, can check my information with others, and so forth.

I may, on the other hand, understand the question as pointing to the general, *logical* possibility of systematic hallucination, lapse of tongue, etc., which affects all judgments. I cannot seek evidence for this; all evidence is affected by the same possibility. The activity of judging presupposes that I am not subject to such lapses or mistakes. The question "Why should I now suspect that I am hallucinating or am otherwise mistaken?" can only be answered by pointing to evidence relevant to the particular situation and not by pointing to the ever-present logical possibility. The possibility is one thing, and I can always tell a story in which it is realized; suspicion (doubt) is something else, and it requires grounds.[12]

2. One's understanding of a practice (as a practitioner) is not only an understanding of when a proposition is to be held fast and when it is vulnerable to doubt and questioning; it is also an understanding of when a proposition generally held fast is eroded as a rule and when one's general conception of the practice must change.

Thus, one cannot agree completely with Wittgenstein's claim that "if something happened . . . calculated to make me doubtful of my own name, there would certainly also be something that made the grounds of these doubts themselves seem doubtful, and I could therefore decide to retain my old belief" (passage 516). Ordinarily, yes. But there are cases in which it is reasonable to accept the grounds of such doubts and unreasonable to retain the old belief. Persuasive evidence that I am wrong about my name may accumulate to convince me that I have been deranged but am now recovered. Giving up my old belief may be the most reasonable way of fitting together what I now know and of continuing to make judgments. The importance of weighing evidence in these cases is the same as in any empirical determination.

In such passages as 516 Wittgenstein has a particular context in view, one in which all criteria of judgment are eroded. Although this is not

12. See also passages 138, 173.

likely to be the case when I have grounded doubts about my memory or my name, it *may* be the case. Wittgenstein asks us to imagine evidence "that made the most certain thing unacceptable to me," that "made me throw over my most fundamental judgments" (passage 517). He speculates that "if I were contradicted on all sides and told that this person's name was not what I had always known it was (and I use 'know' here intentionally), . . . the foundation of all judging must be taken away from me" (passage 614). He seems to conclude that "I can only make judgments at all because things behave thus and thus (as it were, behave kindly)" (passage 615), but this leaves us with an unresolved question. In a sufficiently inchoate situation would I abandon judging (as Wittgenstein suggests in passage 614) or decide to "stay in the saddle" (passage 616) by "retaining my old belief" (passage 516)? The question is otiose because both alternatives lie on the far side of reasonable choice. What is important is that it is the nature of judging that I never reach this kind of impasse. The nature of judging is to treat recalcitrant evidence conservatively: as the situation in passage 614 or 516 is spelled out in detail, it becomes one in which either the "contradictions" (passage 614) come to be explained, one in which they can safely be rejected, or at least one in which I suspend judgment *on this issue alone* pending further investigation. This is not to say that the inchoate situation in which I stop judging *cannot* be reached, but simply that we have no systematic notion of such a situation. When Wittgenstein asks whether "I can make judgments at all because things behave thus and thus" and claims that "it is always by favour of Nature that one knows something" (passage 505), he ought not to be understood as supposing that we have a clear idea of radical contingency, of things *not* behaving "thus and thus" or of nature not favoring us in general ways.

3. Propositions held fast are impeachable either by evidence of cognitive defect or by evidence that one's "picture of the world" is wrong. A generalized deficiency of the first kind is an erosion of judging capacities per se. Evidence of the second kind forces one to change one's world-picture and, perhaps, one's conception of what counts as evidence.

Taking the second case first, let us suppose (with Wittgenstein) that I was transported to Mars and back in my sleep and cannot begin to explain how this was done. To concede that this may have happened is to revise my expectations about what is physically possible; I need new ways of proceeding in which such untoward events are explicable. What counts as evidence for conclusions about physical events is at best suspended. New criteria are needed.[13] I take it that Wittgenstein is referring to a change in the conception of (criteria of) evidence when he says that "here *once more* there is needed a step like the one taken in relativity theory" (passage 305). It is not enough to say about such untoward hypotheses that "nothing in my picture of the world" speaks in their favor (passage 93), because in such cases I lack "a principle of speaking for or against. . . . I must be able to say what *would* speak for it" (passage 117).

The other kind of example, that in which evidence undermines my ability to trust my present faculties or my memory, is one in which I cannot simply reconstruct criteria of evidence. This is so unless my misgivings can be placed in a more general setting of trust and reliance, as it would be if I were reassured, "You are now hallucinating, but the effects of the drug will wear off." Evidence against my ability to trust cognitive faculties would at the same time be evidence undermining my capacity to treat this or anything else *as* evidence.

Both kinds of cases, then, are ones in which unreasonable doubts become reasonable because our practices no longer work, because experience is recalcitrant. At the same time, as we have seen, there are reasonable and unreasonable ways to respond to recalcitrant experiences, reasonable and unreasonable ways of modifying criteria of evidence. To the extent that this is the case, our modifications of practices are moves within still more general practices.

IMPOSSIBLE DOUBT

At the beginning of this chapter, I discussed the question whether any *p*'s are such that doubt is logically impossible. I listed several criteria, namely, (1) whether *p* is affected by the hypothesis that I have lost my wits or "dreamed the whole thing," (2) whether I can tell a story in which *p* is false, and (3) whether the very idea of finding corroboration

---

13. The change I am describing is analogous to that which Kuhn calls a "paradigm shift."

for p is incompatible with p. In this section I shall consider these criteria and the propositions they seem to identify. I shall also look at the distinction between these propositions and those about which doubt is unreasonable.

Consider the following claims: "There are physical objects," "Objects continue in existence when unperceived," and "Historical time did not begin 100 years ago."

55. So is the *hypothesis* possible, that all the things around us don't exist? Would that not be like the hypothesis of our having miscalculated in all our calculations?

Consider also the "law" of induction. Wittgenstein remarks while it may be "the natural law which our inferring apparently follows . . . , it is not an item in our considerations" (passage 135). It would be nonsense, he suggests, to say, "I know that the law of induction is true" (passage 500). Can I be in the "grip of a delusion" (passage 658) about the law of induction, or about the existence of physical objects, or about the "fact" that objects exist unperceived? These p's are not vulnerable to recalcitrant experiences; they seem transevidentiary and transcontextual. No experiences can be said to undercut them because no experiences can be said to support them.

Consider in particular Wittgenstein's remarks about the supposition that objects continue in existence when not perceived.

119. But can it also be said: Everything speaks for, and nothing against the table's still being there when no one sees it? For what speaks for it?
163. Does anyone ever test whether this table remains in existence when no one is paying attention to it? . . .

Could one test the hypothesis about the table by turning around very quickly and unexpectedly, or by setting up an electric eye, etc.? To think in this way is to misunderstand the hypothesis, which is about a difference no possible experience could expose, which could not, *in principle,* be tested by evidence.

These examples (induction, the conviction that the table remains) illustrate criterion (3); the very idea of finding counterevidence does not apply to these p's. It is important to distinguish this claim from a weaker claim which can be made about some examples discussed in the section "Unreasonable Doubt." It may be impossible at time t for me to determine whether I am hallucinating, but I may find confirmation or disconfirmation for p ("I am hallucinating") by asking others whether they too see the pink elephant, and so forth. The very idea of finding evidence is applicable to p ("I am hallucinating") insofar as the hallucination is determinable.

But what about indeterminable hallucinations? Is it impossible for me to have this doubt, "I am having an indeterminable hallucination"? How does this complicate the distinction between unreasonable and impossible doubt as explained by criterion (3)?

Note that "Perhaps I am hallucinating" refers to at least two different kinds of hypotheses. First, as we have seen, there are determinable hallucinations ("Do you see the pink elephants too?"). Second, there are hallucinations that cannot be found out but that can be fitted to what I know. I may, for example, wake in the night and see a green moon. Or did I dream this? Perhaps I will never and can never know. I can reasonably doubt that this was a waking experience. Thus, the class of things I can actually find out is smaller than the class of things I can reasonably doubt.

Now, staying with examples of dreams and hallucinations, let us distinguish (a) hallucination hypotheses I can actually find out, (b) hallucination (dream) hypotheses I can reasonably make but cannot find out (e.g., whether I saw a green moon), (c) things I cannot reasonably doubt because such hypotheses generally impeach my ability to make judgments (like whether I am dreaming *right now*), and (d) things with regard to which the idea of present or future experiential confirmation is inapplicable, e.g., "My whole life is a dream." The difference between (c) and (d) is important. In case (b), I *actually* have something to contrast the dream with, i.e., that which is not a dream, the actual here and now. In case (c), I *hypothetically* have something to contrast the dream with, i.e., the hypothetical here and now, discoverable ex post facto on waking. Case (d) on the other hand, anticipates no actual or hypothetical experience that I might have. This, then, illustrates the application of criterion (3). Case (d) and not case (c) typifies the set of cases to which the very idea of confirmatory or disconfirmatory experience is inapplicable. And this is one way of setting forth the distinction between unreasonable and impossible doubt.

It will be objected that case (d) is not a case of impossible doubt because one can tell a story in which the described situation is realized. May one not doubt whether he himself is in that situation? Here is John Pollock's story about such a situation.

Suppose that a group of psychologists, biophysicists, and neurologists have constructed an adequate explanation of the neurophysiology of perception, and to test their explanation they take a subject from birth and wire him into a computer which directly stimulates his brain in such a way as to give a coherent, but completely false sequence of sensations. In the subject's own mind he would seem to live out a completely normal life, growing up, making friends, going to school, getting a job, marrying and raising a family, etc. And yet all those years he was really sealed into an experimental apparatus in which he was fed intravenously and never had any contact with the outside world.... How do I know that I am not in the position of the subject of the above experiment? [14]

The coherence of the story depends on my regarding the scientists and their experimental apparatus as real. Their lives are not merely imagined, and the objects of their world are real objects. Were I to suppose they in turn are also the subjects of such experiments, the story collapses; there is then no actual subject in the experiment described by Pollock, only an imagined subject. This shows that case (d) makes sense as a coherent story only in a context in which there is an established contrast between dreamworld and reality.

What application does this have to our criteria for cases of impossible doubt? It shows, for one thing, that we must refine criterion (3), which turns out to be ambiguous. The criterion may mean (3a) that the very idea of *my* finding corroboration for p is inapplicable to p, as a proposition I entertain, or (3b) that the very idea of there being in anyone's experience corroboration for p is inapplicable to p, as a proposition I entertain. An example of (3a) is "I may be the subject of a Pollock type of experiment." An example of (3b) is "Everyone may be the subject of a Pollock

14. John Pollock, *Knowledge and Justification* (Princeton: Princeton University Press, 1974), pp. 3–4.

type of experiment" (or "The law of induction is false" or "There are no physical objects"). We have seen that it is not possible to tell a coherent story in which a (3b) type of hypothesis is realized. The hypothesis that the objects of experience may generally be unreal makes sense only as long as there is assumed to be some context in which there are incontrovertibly real objects.

We are now in a position to discuss the several criteria for cases in which doubt is logically impossible, and also to see why, as Wittgenstein says (passage 454), there is no clear boundary. Hypotheses of type (3b) have two complementary characteristics that lead us to say they are cases in which such doubts are logically impossible. On the one hand there is no hypothetical experiencer who would be in a position to corroborate the hypothesis; the experience of every possible experiencer is impeached by the hypothesis. On the other hand, the hypothesis itself invokes concepts like "dream," "imaginary object," or "illusion," which makes sense only if we have something with which to contrast them, like "wakefulness" or "real object"; the latter terms, in turn, have reference only insofar as we reject the hypothesis. Paradoxically, the terms used in raising the hypothesis presuppose the state of affairs being questioned.

Cases of type (3a) are intermediate ones. Posing the question whether I am the subject of a Pollock type of experiment is not logically impossible, but it is not simply "unreasonable" either. It would be unreasonable (case [c]) if I had no grounds for such doubt, but the character of this hypothesis is that I *can* have no grounds. Cases of type (3a) seem to fall in the unclear boundary of doubts more than unreasonable but not logically impossible.

We can now bring into the discussion criteria (1) and (2) for cases in which doubt is logically impossible. Criterion (1) is that doubt about p is logically impossible where p is not affected by the hypothesis that I have "lost my wits" or "dreamed the whole thing." This criterion is again ambiguous, meaning either (1a) that I anticipate a future state in which I have recovered my wits or am awake or (1b) that I may never be in such a future state, but a story can be told in which my wits are in such disarray, etc. Obviously, criterion (1b) coincides with criterion (3a); both are illustrated by coherent Pollock-type hypotheses. Criterion (1a) demarcates simple cases of unreasonable doubt (case [c] again) in which

I hypothesize having grounds for doubt at a future time. Moreover, criterion (2) identifies the shared feature that distinguishes (1b) and (3a) cases from (3b) cases, the feature that I can tell a story about imaginable experiences of hypothetical persons in which p is demonstrably false. If I cannot do this, doubt is logically impossible.

Note, in conclusion, that the attempt to distinguish cases of unreasonable doubt, cases of impossible doubt, and cases in which doubt is in principle unresolvable by me but resolvable by hypothetical others (the important intermediate cases) rests on the unclear notion of being able to tell an intelligible story about imaginable experiences. The following examples show how unclear this is. Is "$2 \times 2 = 4$" transcontextually true and a proposition about which doubt is logically impossible? What about "Consciousness is lodged in bodies"? The answer seems to depend on whether we can describe coherent experiences of a world in which 2 times 2 is not 4 and in which consciousness is disembodied. The burden is, perhaps, on those who claim to be able to tell such stories, and one job of philosophers, it seems, is to determine their coherence. In a story about disembodied consciousness, one can ask for many details. Would the consciousnesses have location in space? How would location be determined? Could location be changed? Could it be changed at will? Can such consciousnesses will other things? Can they give effect to their will? How? The difficulties of constructing such stories are hard to overestimate.

Six

On Conceptual Diversity and Conceptual Change

UNDERSTANDING AND DISAGREEMENT

In chapters one through five I argued that to say that persons understand one another, particularly that they understand one another's
claims to know and to offer grounds, is to say that they have shared
practices. The various things that persons say have meaning as
"moves" within a practice. The role and logical status of what is said
are mutually recognized.

It follows that disagreements are to be understood as understandable
disagreements: to have a disagreement, persons must already be engaged
in a shared practice. They must have not only a shared vocabulary but
also shared assumptions about what sorts of grounds are relevant to what
sorts of claims, as well as some shared beliefs about which no doubt can
"possibly" occur.[1] This does not mean that all understandable disagreement is resolvable disagreement. Resolution will probably not be forth-
coming when there is disagreement about what particular matters are
relevant to particular conclusions, or about how much weight to assign
particular pieces of evidence, or whenever parties have inconclusive evidence. Obviously, the notion of a shared practice is elastic and inexact,
and necessarily so. It is the notion that persons may have shared critical
standards and yet, to some extent, use them differently. A determination

1. See chapter five.

of what is a shared standard used differently and what is a different standard can only be made case by case.

However elastic it is, the notion may be attacked on grounds other than vagueness. It may be said that we understand persons in many situations in which we do not have shared practices, shared ways of assessing evidence, and so forth. In fact, one of the things we *typically* claim to understand is precisely this: that others have practices in which we do not participate or practices the premises of which we reject, or both. Some examples can be drawn from the history of thought, in particular from the history of science. We claim to understand Aristotle and Newton, and part of what we say we understand is that their conceptions of what counts as evidence, and even of what it means to seek evidence, are irreconcilably different from each other's and from our conceptions. Further, the understanding involved is not reciprocal; we say we understand them but make no assumption that they would understand us. (We may be quite convinced of the opposite.) Our initial characterization of understandable disagreement implied that understanding *is* reciprocal and, therefore, that characterization must be modified.

Another set of difficult counterexamples does not involve change in critical standards over time or the absence of reciprocity. We claim to understand systems of moral practice and belief and religious systems that coexist with our own practices but in which we do not participate or believe. We recognize mutually incompatible alternative practices. Thus, in general, what stands fast for me in different contexts does not stand fast for everyone I claim to be able to understand. What I hold fast may be rejected by others as nonsense. Even more importantly, what stands fast for me here and now may not stand fast for me in the future and may not have done so in the past.

I shall distinguish two questions. First, if my ability to understand is coextensive with my own usages (my practices), how can I say (truthfully) that I understand practices that I reject and in which I do not participate? Second, if one can recognize and understand such alien practices, how may one regard them? Can we have criteria of evaluation that entitle us to say that some practices are better than others, or truer than others, or more advanced than others?

In this chapter I shall try to answer both questions, drawing in part on *On Certainty*. It is clear that the first question has priority over the second: we cannot evaluate what we cannot understand.

THE LIMITS OF UNDERSTANDING

The first problem is one of setting limits. Not every odd saying is understandable; not all aberrant behavior, including aberrant verbal behavior, can be understood as part of a coherent, if different, way of thinking. How do we delimit the set of experiences that are evidence of alien practices?

Wittgenstein observes that someone who claimed not to know whether he had ever been in China would simply not make sense unless, for example, he had reason to think he might have been there. Perhaps he was once near the Chinese border (passage 333). If someone said that he did not know whether he had a body, "I should take him to be a half-wit. But I shouldn't know what it would mean to try to convince him that he had one" (passage 257). Similarly, if someone is persistently wrong about the address at which he has lived for many years, one would not know what to make of his error (passage 67). In each case what is missing is an understandable relation between the speaker and his ignorance, his doubt, or his error. And in such cases it is not possible to see his state as ignorance, doubt, or mistake properly so-called.[2]

Each of these examples shows how much stage setting is needed before one can fit a verbal claim (or more generally, any piece of behavior) into a framework of procedures and assumptions attributable to the claimant. The various examples are not indisputably nonsense, but they are nonsense until a context is offered, until we know what kind of experience would be regarded as counting for or against the claim. In Wittgenstein's familiar example, "the earth has not long existed" may be a scientific claim (involving scientific evidence), a historical claim, or perhaps a mystical claim (passage 236). "This mountain didn't exist a year ago" may be rebutted by geological and historical facts in some contexts, but

2. See also passages 106, 108, 255, 258.

not if the intended meaning is "This mountain didn't exist a year ago, but an exactly similar one did" (passage 237). Such claims are inchoate; we demand more contextual information to understand them.[3]

Cases that we despair of understanding show how special are those cases which we recognize as claiming, doubting, or making a mistake in different practices from our own. We need a hypothesis about what is being doubted or about how such mistakes arise and can be corrected. It seems we can form and apply such hypotheses about moral, scientific, religious, or other beliefs that we do not share, but this is not yet so in the passages quoted above. I can, for example, understand how a medieval psychologist may doubt and confirm claims about personality based on a theory of humors.

Thus, the naked claim that "we don't know how one gets to the moon, but those who get there know at once that they are there" does not challenge and offer an alternative to "our whole system of physics." An alternative physics would explain how such things were possible in a system that explained the more ordinary events of experience as well. The explanation would not (we are assuming) be one that we would accept or that would be familiar to us, but it would (as in the case of the psychology of humors) have to be recognizable as an explanation and a system. We feel less "distant" from medieval cosmologists (from whose theories we can predict their conclusions and observations) than we do from the person whose claims and other behavior seem simply inchoate.

We saw in chapter five that we would be bewildered by someone who denied the law of induction, or denied that there were physical objects, or suggested that all our calculations have been wrong. This is so because such assertions cannot, however we try, be fitted into unfamiliar practices; they are incompatible with proceeding in any intelligible way.

(Wittgenstein regularly calls inexplicable behavior of various kinds "mental disturbance." Wittgenstein notwithstanding, when disturbance is functional and not organic, such behavior has its own consistency and is explicable as a response to situations as they are perceived by the actor. Such behavior can be fitted in a consistently aberrant pattern. In contrast,

3. See also passage 259.

the behavior examined in this section is not yet part of a coherent pattern.) [4]

We can now turn to cases of very general systems of belief that we recognize as coherent practices different from our own. Thus, Wittgenstein reminds us of tribes that have judged that a king can make rain (passage 132) or that oracles can be consulted to anticipate the future (passage 609). He asks whether we are justified in saying that such peoples judge wrongly, whether we are not thus using "our language-game as a base from which to *combat* theirs?" (passage 609).

To confront *these* alien practices is to recognize them *as* practices with understandable and predictable procedures. Oracles and ordeal by fire are recognizable as systematic resources used to find things out. What is involved in saying that these practices are more or less "correct" than our own? Are we entitled to say that they are wrong?

I shall argue that two very different (and incompatible) responses to these questions can be found in Wittgenstein. The first response, which is *readily* found in Wittgenstein, leads to unsatisfactory conclusions. It is a clear-cut argument, easily outlined, and it proceeds as follows: We can call matters "right" and "wrong" insofar as we have shared procedures for determining what is right and what is wrong. This does not mean that in sharing a practice we will be able to resolve all disagreement or agree about the weight of every piece of evidence, but it does mean that we must share general criteria for what counts as evidence. Where there are significant differences between different persons' criteria, different but internally consistent systems of reaching conclusions, there is no ground for claiming that one way of proceeding is right in itself or closer to being right than another. At most, one can reject a different system and adhere to one's own system, but to do so is not to make a grounded decision. If, for example, I try to offer grounds by showing that the oracle or the rainmaking dance is statistically unreliable, the adherent of these prac-

4. Compare the fuller discussion of these issues in chapter two.

tices will reply that this is irrelevant. He will say that I have not proved that there is no connection between the oracle and events, etc., but only that the gods are capricious. Both I and the tribesman claim to derive our ways of proceeding from experience, and neither of us can ground his preference by appeal to independent criteria of decision. Recall that Wittgenstein makes clear the absence of such criteria when he says that "we may derive [ways of judging] from experience, but experience does not direct us to derive anything from experience. . . . [W]e do not have a ground for seeing this in turn as a ground" (passage 130).

If the rainmaker and I have such different practices, I cannot give him grounds (which he will see as grounds) for abandoning his beliefs. I may convert him to my beliefs and procedures, but I cannot do so by giving grounds.

611. Where two principles really do meet which cannot be reconciled with one another, then each man declares the other a fool and heretic.

It seems to be Wittgenstein's view that the missionary converts natives not by giving reasons but, having exhausted reasons, by "persuasion" (passage 612). Similarly, someone who disabused a king of the belief that the world began with his birth would not be bringing the king around to the "right" view on the basis of reasons, but would be "converting" the king, bringing him "to look at the world in a different way" (passage 92).[5] I may induce such a conversion by representing my view as simple, symmetrical, or comprehensive, but this is not a *reason* why my picture is "right" (passage 92). Nor is there an independent standard of simplicity or comprehensiveness. The rainmaker's notion of a capricious god may be simpler than my meteorological determinations; the concept of a *materia universalis* may be as comprehensive as any concept in my picture. Nonetheless, it may be the case that *when* conversion occurs, it occurs because the adopted theory is *thought* by the convertee to have one or another such advantage as greater comprehensiveness, greater simplicity, etc.

Individuals use oracles, believe in capricious gods, or disbelieve in beings that they cannot perceive because they have been taught to make

5. See also passages 262, 264.

judgments in certain ways. Judgments are possible, we have seen, insofar as certain judgments are held fast.

144. The child learns to believe a host of things. I.e. it learns to act according to these beliefs. Bit by bit there forms a system of what is believed, and in that system some things stand unshakeably fast and some are more or less liable to shift. What stands fast does so, not because it is intrinsically obvious or convincing; it is rather held fast by what lies around it.[6]

The judgment that there are capricious gods and that they must be placated is the kind of principle which governs action and thought in a general way and is generally held fast.

Let us stand back from this argument and evaluate it. It is obviously true that I may discover and recognize internally consistent ways of thinking and investigating which are incompatible with my own practices. I may or may not be able to offer arguments that the other person will recognize as reasons for preferring my practices. If our ways are very different, many of my reasons will predictably be rejected. It is also true that he and I proceed as we do and believe in the reliability of our practices in part because we learned to do so. (But to say that this is the cause is not to say it is the reason we follow our practices.) The observation that there is no objective and independent standpoint available to either of us from which to evaluate competing practices was discussed and explained in chapters one and three: "experience does not direct us to derive anything from experience" (passage 130). Experience is not an independent ground from which to judge practices.

These observations, let us assume, are uncontroversial, but do they support the conclusions of the argument we are now evaluating? One such conclusion is that I am not entitled to call the oracle consulter unreasonable or to claim that his practice is wrong. He is reasonable insofar as he follows his practices as scrupulously as I follow mine. Accordingly, his practice is not wrong but only different; to be entitled to call him "wrong" I must be able to show that he misapplies shared and accepted procedures, but clearly he and I do not share relevant procedures. Thus, divergent, ongoing practices are generally not to be called more or less reasonable. Just as this is true of me and the oracle consulter, it is *pro*

---

6. See also passages 140, 141, 142.

tanto true of Aristotle and Einstein, a Buddhist and a Christian, a theist and an atheist, an egalitarian and an elitist. The question of justifying one way of proceeding in the face of another cannot arise because there is no shared framework in which the activity of judging and justifying can proceed.

These conclusions fly in the face of many ordinary assumptions and experiences. From the fact that I "inherited" my practices it does not follow that I cannot have and give compelling grounds for my "preference." The existence of a cause does not preclude my having reasons. My being able to justify my rejection of oracle consulting does not seem to depend on whether the mistaken oracle consulter can or cannot understand my justification. Moreover, when the consulter abandons his practice and is converted to the practices of modern science, such "conversion" or "persuasion" does not seem altogether different from the outcome of reasoning from some common ground. In fact, given the divergence that the argument assumes, conversion would (implausibly) seem to be an altogether capricious event.

Can we say that the diversity between the theist and the atheist, the egalitarian and the elitist, the Buddhist and the Christian is genuine disagreement and that each comes to understand and reject the other's position by using a shared practice which makes possible such understanding? To answer this, we must reconsider what counts as a shared practice. There seem to be three possible conclusions we could reach. If we accept the general argument (which we are in the process of evaluating), we can say that the theist and the atheist, etc., share the same practices and can judge each other *or* that they do not share the same practices and cannot judge each other. If, however, we find grounds for rejecting the general argument, we may be able to say that they do not share the same relevant practices but can nonetheless judge each other comparatively. This third possibility is attractive because (1) the divergences at issue seem to be paradigm cases of unshared practices and (2) it seems correct to say that a preference for, say, experimentation over oracle consulting is reasoned, defensible, and justifiable.

If we reject the proffered general argument, we may also try to accommodate some other complications that do not seem accountable by the general argument. For example, I regard Newton as reasonable, but would not regard a Newtonian in the twentieth century as reasonable. I regard certain moral positions with which I disagree as reasonable and reject others as unreasonable. On occasion, I will question whether *I* have proceeded reasonably. Thus, the view that I can only make judgments of reasonableness within my own practice, using unmodifiable standards, is simply false to experience. All of these points reinforce the view that the argument, as given, is inadequate.

I shall consider in the next section a more satisfactory analysis of divergences in thought and practice. Before doing so, I shall summarize the experiences which such an analysis must explain.

1. If someone in my own society believes that he can read his future in tea leaves, I will say he is wrong and offer him reasons that I expect him to recognize as reasons and that may or may not persuade him to give up his practice. If he persists and gives no reasons that *I* can recognize as reasons, I will say that he is unreasonable. If I find someone in an alien culture who has exactly the same belief, I will have exactly the same reasons for saying he is wrong, reasons which may or may not be intelligible to him. Whether he understands my reasons and whether many others in his society do what he does are irrelevant to my belief that his way of going about things is wrong and to my conviction that I have good reasons for thinking this.

2. I will, let us assume, think of an alien practice as one in which certain *kinds* of reasons that I offer will be rejected out of hand because of beliefs held fast. One example is that of an "ultimate" belief in a capricious god. But if I ascribe this kind of closure to an alien practice, how can I imagine such a practitioner *ever* recognizing recalcitrant experiences and changing his ways of proceeding? And if I do not conceive of him changing in understandable ways, how do I account for "conversion"? More importantly, what right do I have for claiming that my practices can change and that I can recognize recalcitrant experiences when I deny these capacities to others? How is it that *I* ever come to reject some of my inherited beliefs and claim to do so in reasoned ways? The fact of change suggests that the model of practices as closed must be rejected in principle.

3. I can imagine myself converting an oracle consulter into a man of modern science by introducing him to methods and resources (technol-

ogies, terms, etc.) that I have and he lacks. Such examples of conversion can be documented. I call him primitive because I have resources that are unfamiliar to him and because, let us suppose, he has no resources that are unfamiliar to me. I cannot imagine he will convert me into a consulter of oracles, and as a matter of sociological fact, this kind of conversion rarely happens. It is not impossible, but it is more than unlikely, that he will be able to introduce me to matters which can be explained by appeal to his resources and not by mine. It is not at all unlikely (there is ample precedent) that I will be able to introduce him to such matters. If he insists that his scheme explains more, he will offer either *explananda* that I cannot explain or dismiss, and I will then no longer regard him as primitive, or *explananda* that I can explain and dismiss, in which case I will fail to understand the grounds of his insistence.

I regard the prize-winning chemist who insists that the eucharistic wine is the blood of Christ in a very different way from the oracle consulter. I do not think that the chemist will give up his claim if I show him what I know. The suggestion that we must treat all nonshared practices indifferently and nonevaluatively cannot take account of our different attitudes to primitive and to sophisticated practices, nor does it explain our expectations in encounters with so-called primitive ones. I shall now sketch a view of divergent practices which takes account of these experiences.

THE PERSPECTIVE OF ONE'S OWN PRACTICE

We have seen that in some instances of divergence in practices and beliefs, the divergence is irreducible, and attempts at conversion will be unavailing. For example, a devout Christian may disagree with the proposition that every human being has two human parents and say that Jesus is a counterexample. A Catholic may contend that wine in certain circumstances is transubstantiated as the blood of Jesus (passage 239). Moreover, "very intelligent and well-educated people believe in the story of creation in the Bible, while others hold it as proven false, and the grounds of the latter are well known to the former" (passage 336).

In these cases all "facts" known to one party are known to the other, but *some* facts and procedures affirmed by one are denied by the other.

The Catholic who believes in transubstantiation does not deny the chemist's facts about wafers and wine, but he holds some facts to be true on the basis of resources which the chemist rejects. Each knows the nature of the other's grounds and the other's conception of evidence, and each believes that the other can offer him no troublesome arguments as to why he is wrong. Coexistence and interaction of the Catholic with the chemist are possible to the extent that there is much that they share in the face of this disagreement. Indeed, their shared conception of ordinary genetics and ordinary chemistry makes it possible for them to understand and express their disagreement, its nature and limits. The disagreement is "fixed" and any change of position involves not so much a weighing of new evidence as an alteration of a conception of evidence, i.e., a conversion.[7]

To what extent is the relationship between the chemist and the Catholic generalizable to other examples of conflicting practices? Note that in this case there is a stable impasse because each understands all claims and procedures of the other. Rejection of one another's views presupposes understanding. It misrepresents the situation to say that the two *mean* different things by what they say simply because they have different beliefs and procedures; they share meanings insofar as they share usages. When one affirms and the other denies that *this* is blood, they are *using* words in the same way and they mean the same things by them.

Note that there is ambiguity in the claim, "If the Catholic and the chemist have different practices, they must mean different things by the word 'blood.'" The claim is true insofar as one and not the other will apply "blood" to the wine in some contexts. It is not true insofar as they both apply the word to the wine in the same context when one affirms and the other denies that *this* is blood.

The same ambiguity haunts such passages as this:

65. When language-games change, then there is a change in concepts, and with the concepts the meanings of words change.

If I become converted to Catholicism and begin to affirm what I now deny, do the meanings of my words change so that what I now affirm

7. See passages 645, 646, 647.

has a different meaning than what I then denied? To say this seems needlessly paradoxical; it implies wrongly that the chemist is not denying what the Catholic affirms.

The situation of the Catholic and the chemist is atypical among examples of so-called different conceptual frameworks. If we consider the situation of the oracle follower vis-à-vis the modern scientist, or of the Ptolemaic astronomer vis-à-vis the modern astronomer, we have a different situation, more clearly asymmetrical in understanding.[8] Our attitude, Wittgenstein suggests, is inevitably this: "Let them be never so sure of their belief—they are wrong and we know it" (passage 286). He concludes that *we* are convinced that "if we compare our system of knowledge with theirs then theirs is evidently the poorer one by far" (passage 286), and we buttress this view with the conviction that "we belong to a community which is bound together by science and education" (passage 298).

While these passages are open to various interpretations, I shall argue for the following account. To say in particular cases that their system of knowledge is "poorer by far" and that we are "bound together by science and education" is to say that whenever I can *say* what they believe I am in a situation in which my usages (my meanings) embrace and include theirs. Understanding and evaluating their beliefs *presuppose* that I can say what they believe, and say it (of course) in my own words, with my own concepts. Once I have said what *they* think, I will either recognize in their observations recalcitrant data for my own ways of thinking, or I will use what I think about the same matters as a measure of what is wrong or right in their thought. In this sense their system is poorer: what

8. I have been assuming without argument that the nonreligious person who denies that the wine is the blood of Christ can be said to understand the religious claim. I think we must reject any analysis of "understanding x" such that the criterion for understanding x is believing that x is true, for this would preclude the possibility of understanding a claim and holding it to be false. More generally, an adequate analysis of understanding will show how it is possible for two persons to understand a proposition and disagree on its truth value. The blood/wine passage (239) in *On Certainty* suggests that Wittgenstein's analysis of understanding would be unsatisfactory in this way.

I hold true is inevitably (as a matter of logic) [9] my measure for what is true in what they hold.

It is obviously not an objection to passage 286 that we learn from others; learning requires and presupposes that within our own way of thinking we can recognize recalcitrant or unexplained experience. Perhaps the Ptolemaic astronomer cannot learn directly from the modern astronomer because he cannot experience the same things as data. But perhaps he can learn through intermediaries, in effect recapitulating the history of astronomy. Accordingly, Wittgenstein says that we learn only from someone to whom we are bound together by science and education, who knows what we know and more. This means that the teacher shares all of the relevant usages of the learner and has other usages as well, and that he can display a relationship between the old (shared) ones and the new. To the extent that one learns, one comes to adopt a system. The reason we call certain people and systems "primitive" is that we cannot learn from them in this sense. We can represent their beliefs and procedures to ourselves, but they cannot apprehend our own. (They *may* of course think about us in precisely the same way as we think of them, if they think of our ways as understandable at all. Passage 286 says that insofar as I see their—or they see my—system as *different, each* will see the *other's* as poorer in this sense.)

What significance do these reflections about the relation of understanding to evaluation in regard to alien systems have for my attitude toward my own system?

595. "But I can still imagine someone making all these connexions, and none of them corresponding with reality. Why shouldn't I be in a similar case?"

If I imagine such a person I also imagine a reality, a world that surrounds him; and I imagine him as thinking (and speaking) in contradiction to this world.

Wittgenstein then refers to our certainty that water boils at 100°C, a fact that we have tested in school, that appears in basic school-texts, etc. May this certainty fail to correspond with reality?

9. See discussion of logic in chapter two.

599. ...—Now one can offer counter-examples ... which show that human beings have held this and that to be certain which later, according to our opinion, proved false. *But the argument is worthless. To say: in the end we can only adduce such grounds as we hold to be grounds, is to say nothing at all.*

   I believe that at the bottom of this is a misunderstanding of the nature of our language-games. (emphasis added)
606. That to my mind someone else has been wrong is no ground for assuming that I am wrong now. —But isn't it a ground for assuming that I *might* be wrong? It is *no* ground for any *unsureness* in my judgment, or my actions.

These passages are among the most important in *On Certainty*. Here Wittgenstein is clearest about the consequences of the asymmetry between one's own ways of thinking about one's own procedures and one's ways of thinking about the ways of thinking of others. In referring to asymmetry as a fact I do not mean simply that my ways of thinking are mine, which is tautological, nor that I will see alien ways as "poorer by far," which may be false—as in the case of the confrontation with the Catholic. I mean rather that, in the absence of a recognition of recalcitrant experience, I will use what I hold true as the measure of what is true in the beliefs of others. To understand the oracle consulter or the Catholic, each of us employs his own ways of thinking and judging. To regard the oracle consulter as thinking in contradistinction to this world is *the same thing as* regarding him as thinking in contradistinction to my way of thinking. I cannot ask and make a coherent judgment about whether my own "connexions" correspond with reality (passage 595). For me to question my world-picture in this way is *already* for me to disown it in the face of a new conviction about how things are. (Of course another person *can* regard me as thinking in contradistinction to this world.)

   Presented with what others offer as grounds, I can give reasons which satisfy me, whether or not they satisfy (or are intelligible to) those particular other persons, for rejecting grounds of this kind. The fact that others proceed differently (to my mind, wrongly) is no *evidence* at all that I am wrong; it is not the sort of thing that counts as evidence. In the same way, the *possibility* of coming upon recalcitrant experiences is not the sort of thing that can dislodge my confidence. Wittgenstein invites us to imagine events "really unheard-of," like cattle standing on their heads and conversing, or trees changing slowly into persons and persons into trees, or water freezing at temperatures high enough for boiling. These unrealized imaginings are powerless to show us that we are wrong or to show that our judgments are mistakes (passages 513, 558).

558. ... Whatever may happen in the future, however water may behave in the future,—we *know* that up to now it has behaved *thus* in innumerable instances.

This fact is fused into the foundations of our language-game.

The point here is not psychological but logical. A condition of thinking about any alien ways of thinking, or about possible recalcitrant experiences, is to have a way of thinking which is not alien and within which one is confident that such recalcitrant experiences will not occur. One's own way of thinking is one's only resource for recognizing the behavior of others as "giving grounds" or as "making judgments," and it is one's only measure for truth and falsity. To say that *p* is true for someone else, someone who makes judgments in a recognizably different way, is no basis at all for my saying that it is true, partly true, or something I cannot judge. The concepts one uses to describe alien ways of thinking are one's own concepts; one's attitude toward the truth and falsity of the beliefs of others is determined by one's own criteria for what is true. The question whether one's own point of view *ought* to have this role is really the nonsensical question whether what *I* call judgment and evidence are *really* judgment and evidence.

The hypothesis that I can assess (from some independent standpoint) my own practices (my own ways of thinking and judging), that I can hold them in abeyance, and that I *ought* to do so, involves two misconceptions about the asymmetry between one's own practices and those of others.

1. As we saw in chapter four, we never say of others, from colleagues to aborigines, that what they say or claim to know *must* be the case. The assurance of the most trustworthy of persons, Wittgenstein reminds us, does not guarantee that he knows, but only "that he believes he knows"

(passage 137).[10] With others I can always demand grounds and in principle assess whatever grounds are proffered. I inevitably see the claims of others as *personal* testimony and I can always ask why I should believe what another person believes.

174. I act with *complete* certainty. But this certainty is my own.

It is a fallacy to say that because my claims, as seen by *others*, are "merely" personal and because "my certainty is my own," I ought to (or can) subject my own ways of proceeding to the same kind of scrutiny and evaluation as I do the claims of others. This is nonsense: what could I use to check my picture of the world and my practices as a whole but my picture of the world and my practices?[11] The recommendation that I treat my own claims as merely personal is incoherent. It involves the misconception that I can stand impartial between my own ways of proceeding and those of others. (Of course, I may well question whether I have grounds for particular empirical beliefs within my system, but doing so presupposes that I do not question whether what I am looking for are the sorts of things which *count* as grounds.)

Accordingly, my attitude toward my own practices and my own convictions is unavoidably this:

436. Is God bound by our knowledge? Are a lot of our statements *incapable* of falsehood? For that is what we want to say.
623. What is odd is that in such a case I always feel like saying (although it is wrong): "I know that—so far as one can know such a thing." That is incorrect, but something right is hidden behind it.
578. But mightn't a higher authority assure me that I don't know the truth? So that I had to say "Teach me!"? But then my eyes would have to be opened.

We "want to say" that "God [is] bound by our knowledge" because the possibility of higher authority is one which *cannot* count in our reasoning. I can admit the possibility that I will come to think differently (that "my eyes" will be "opened") but I cannot accommodate this standing possibility ("so far as one can know such a thing") by disclaiming my own certainty.

10. See passages 13, 14, 22.
11. See discussion of realism in chapter two.

Saying "I cannot be wrong" and "That cannot be false" does not and cannot have the consequence that I or others will *never* "correctly" abandon what is claimed.

652. Now can I prophesy that men will never throw over the present arithmetical propositions, never say that now at last they know how the matter stands? Yet would that justify a doubt on our part?

And this yields a philosophically important general conclusion about practices: we claim, *not wrongly*, that some of our beliefs are universal (or universally true) and yet we cannot guess whether these beliefs will themselves be given up.

559. You must bear in mind that the language-game is so to speak something unpredictable. I mean: it is not based on grounds. It is not reasonable (or unreasonable).

It is there—like our life.

440. There is something universal here; not just something personal.

We have seen that the possibility of change cannot be expressed by "I might be wrong," which has its use when a mistake can be fitted with other things about which I am not mistaken. My attitude that my own notions of judgment and evidence (my own ways of proceeding) are universally applicable and that alien notions (Aristotelian scientific beliefs and procedures, mystical beliefs and procedures, etc.) are matters to be evaluated to determine whether they offer experiences recalcitrant to my way of understanding, is not *merely* an attitude. It is (as we say) a "logical" condition of making judgments and using "true" and "false."

404. I want to say: it's not that on some points men know the truth with perfect certainty. No: perfect certainty is only a matter of their attitude.

405. *But of course there is still a mistake even here.* (emphasis added)

Men do not "know the truth with perfect certainty" because there remains a series of impotent possibilities—possibilities because they cannot be discounted, because life is unpredictable, impotent because the awareness of their possibility is not the sort of thing I can weigh as evidence for or against any grounded beliefs.

642. But suppose someone produced the scruple: what if I suddenly as it

were woke up and said "Just think, I've been imagining I was called L. W!"
—well, who says that I don't wake up once again and call *this* an extraordinary fancy, and so on? [12]

New and recalcitrant experiences will make me alter my ways of thinking and judging to accommodate them before I admit incoherence. Even seeing myself as crazy is, as a last resort, a way of attributing coherence through a universal world-picture; I do so in this case by abdicating from my own ways of judging altogether and deferring to those whom I hold to be sane and whose judgments can be trusted. "If that is wrong then I am crazy" is not an argument that I am not crazy, but it describes the nature and depth of my conviction; it is said perhaps to persuade but, more importantly, to characterize the consequences for me of conceding error.

2. The first misconception is that we can (and ought to) take the same critical posture toward our own ways of judging and our own world-picture as we take to those of others and as others take toward ours. A second relevant misconception is that, since we can doubt and justify some of our beliefs, we ought to be able to doubt and justify all of them indiscriminately. This is the point at which we began our inspection of *On Certainty* in chapter one. Doubting and being wrong occur within practices, and doubting requires that some beliefs (which constitute the practice) not be doubted, not be the sort of thing which can be doubted. Those important practices which I have called "knowing-games" are held as universal in application in this sense: to be an initiate into such a practice is to apply the same standards of judging to all that is understood, including the alien practices and criteria of others.

To conclude, I have tried to show that my encounters with the oracle follower, the Catholic, and the Ptolemaic astronomer involve matters which I will understand, if at all, through my own concepts and which I will judge by my own criteria of judging truth and falsity. My tools of understanding may be used badly or well; there is good and bad history of science, good and bad philology, but I cannot judge that my tools are *inherently* inadequate for the task. The oracle follower and the Ptolemaic

12. See also passages 223, 557, 668.

astronomer will, it is likely but not certain, offer no experiences which I cannot comfortably accommodate (or think so, which comes to the same thing). I may convert them to my way of thinking, and they may convert me to theirs; that is unpredictable. But in applying my concepts to understand their behavior and thought, I affirm the power and universality of those concepts.

Seven

On Philosophy

In what sense is doing philosophy itself a practice with its own methods and moves? Often, Wittgenstein takes the strong position that philosophical utterances are nonmoves in any practice. In *Tractatus Logico-Philosophicus,* his earliest work, he says

Most of the propositions and questions to be found in philosophical works are not false but nonsensical. Consequently we cannot give any answer to questions of this kind, but can only establish that they are nonsensical. Most of the propositions and questions of philosophers arise from our failure to understand the logic of our language. (Proposition 4.003)

And in *Philosophical Investigations* he observes that

the confusions which occupy us arise when language is like an engine idling, not when it is doing work....

...the clarity that we are aiming at is indeed *complete* clarity. But this simply means that the philosophical problems should *completely* disappear.[1]

Finally, in *On Certainty* we find Wittgenstein saying that those propositions to which we return "as if bewitched," those "that don't get us any further," should be "expunged" from use (passages 31, 33).

A frequent theme in Wittgenstein's writings is that certain philosoph-

1. *PI,* part 1, paragraphs 132, 133.

ical problems are to be dissolved rather than solved and that certain philosophical propositions (or claims made by philosophers) are non-sense and therefore must be "expunged." (An example seems to be Moore's claim, "I know this is my hand.") Does this mean (1) that there is no distinctive job for philosophy except to reveal its own nonsense and that, as Wittgenstein says, philosophy "leaves everything as it is" [2] and "neither explains nor deduces anything"? [3] Or does it mean (2) that the distinctive job of philosophy has often been misconceived and that philo-sophical explanations are of a distinctive kind, not to be confused with other sorts of investigations? According to the second view, a more mod-est critique than the first, the mistake of Moore and the nonsense of phi-losophers generally come from a confused conception, and a confused doing, of their job, not from attempting to do a job in the first place. I shall try to explain and defend (2); I shall also try to show that many passages in *On Certainty* support this view.

In discussing Wittgenstein's use of the term "logic" in chapter two, I referred to those special contexts in which persons step back from familiar circumstances of speaking, thinking, and acting to describe and investi-gate those circumstances. Sometimes persons have occasion to understand and explain what they do by describing the sorts of things which we have called "practices." One may or may not call such reflective investigations "philosophy," but it seems appropriate to do so. It is, in any case, im-portant that there are such investigations and that performing such in-vestigations itself constitutes a practice; that is, the claims made by such investigators (by philosophers) are to be understood in a distinctive way. If the claims of philosophers are a kind of practice, an account of prac-tices in general must also explain *this* kind of practice. In *Philosophical Investigations*, Wittgenstein says accordingly

One might think: if philosophy speaks of the use of the word "philosophy" there must be a second-order philosophy. But it is not so: it is, rather, like the case of orthography, which deals with the word "orthography" among others without then being second-order. [4]

2. *PI*, part 1, paragraph 124.
3. *PI*, part 1, paragraph 126.
4. *PI*, part 1, paragraph 121.

In other words, what I called in chapter two "metapropositions" are also propositions, and this kind of practice of self-scrutiny in thought and action is itself a practice with distinctive procedures, a practice which can be done badly or well.

The same point can be made differently. It would be consistent with position (1) that philosophers, in "leaving everything as it is," may only quote or cite what ordinary persons, ordinary "practitioners," say. The distinction here is the familiar one between use and mention: the position to be examined as (1) is whether philosophers can only mention how language is used rather than use language in a characteristic way themselves. This is to be contrasted with the position that there is an appropriate and distinctively philosophical way of making the points which Moore is trying to make and making badly. To say better what Moore intended to say is to engage in the practice of philosophy and to use language for a particular purpose; it is not merely to mention the uses which distinguish other, nonreflective practices. This latter position is position (2), and I shall try to explain it.

IDEALISM AND REALISM AS PHILOSOPHY

When Wittgenstein calls philosophy "nonsense" in *On Certainty,* his examples are realism and idealism. He says that Moore is a realist and that Moore tries to prove that skeptical idealism is false. By looking at these examples, we can clarify what Wittgenstein sees as philosophy and what he sees as Moore's mistake.

Wittgenstein gives as an example of the idealist's inquiry the question, "What right have I not to doubt the existence of my hand?" His own response is that a doubt of this kind "only works in a language-game" and that, to the extent that we do not know what the idealist's doubt is like, we do not understand his question (passage 24). But Wittgenstein acknowledges that the idealist is not dealing with practical doubt; the idealist holds that "there is a further doubt *behind* that one.—That this is an illusion has to be shewn [*sic*] in a different way" (passage 19). He notes that Moore fails to appreciate this distinction and therefore equates skeptical doubt with practical doubt, conflating doubts about the existence of my hand with doubts about the existence of the planet Saturn (passage 20).

Wittgenstein's point is that when the idealist claims that perhaps there are no physical objects, it is not responsive to say, "I know that this is my hand." The idealist as skeptic does not claim to doubt existence in the same sense in which doubts about existence are determinable in knowing-games. Moore, according to Wittgenstein, assumes that the idealist's kind of doubt is the familiar and determinable kind; thus, he claims that by refuting doubt about his hand, he has refuted doubt about the external world; by refuting doubt about the external world, he has proved realism. Accordingly, Wittgenstein says that Moore "has every right" to say, for example, that he knows that this is his hand, but his saying so and his being right or wrong *cannot* be of "philosophical importance," i.e., of importance in the debate with the skeptic. "If Moore is attacking those who say that one cannot really know such a thing, he can't do it by assuring them that *he* knows this and that" (passage 520).

There are two putative uses for "I know this is my hand," two uses which are incompatible and which Moore fails to distinguish. The first is as a move in a knowing-game, a promissory note for giving grounds. But for Moore to use the proposition in this way would be doubly misguided, for Moore is *not* really claiming to be able to give *further* grounds for "I know that this is my hand," and he misunderstands the skeptic as engaged in a familiar knowing-game. The second use is for the purpose of pointing to the role of the conviction in knowing-games, i.e., as a matter which it makes no sense to question or ground (except in extraordinary circumstances). In the latter case, "I know that this is my hand" is, we have seen, a *logical* insight.[5]

59. "I know" is here a *logical* insight. Only realism can't be proved by means of it.

Logical insights are not the sorts of things that *prove* anything, for they are not moves within knowing-games, not ways of giving grounds for claims.

What then is Wittgenstein's notion of philosophy as practiced variously by skeptical idealists and by Moore? First, Wittgenstein agrees with the skeptic that Moore's argument is not responsive as a countermove

5. See chapter two.

within a knowing-game; Moore is mistaken if that is what he is trying to do. Wittgenstein and the skeptic are in agreement that so-called skeptical doubt does not infect practice. Illustrating this, Wittgenstein himself raises a skeptical puzzle by asking, "Everything speaks for, and nothing against the table's still being there when no one sees it? For what does speak for it?" (passage 119). He responds, however, that if anyone were to doubt it, his doubt could not arise in practice; as a practical matter we could "peacefully leave him to doubt it, since it makes no difference at all" (passage 120).[6] But Wittgenstein knows that this response is inadequate as a response to skepticism. It is Moore's skeptic, and not Wittgenstein's skeptic, who is answered by this kind of appeal to practice. As we saw above, the skeptic claims a "further doubt" (see passage 19). Second, Wittgenstein and the skeptic differ, it appears, in thinking that there *is* further doubt, in supposing, for example, that tables may behave unpredictably. But the difference is elusive, if it *is* a difference. In offering passage 119 for consideration, Wittgenstein is *himself* in a sense supposing that tables may vanish, etc., and he is characteristically cautious in his conclusion: one "feels" like saying this cannot be supposed or wouldn't be supposed.

Just as Wittgenstein is accusing Moore of confusing a logical insight with a move within a knowing-game by saying "I know . . . ," he is similarly accusing the skeptic of harboring the illusion that a logical insight can properly be expressed by talking of personally doubting, which also appears to be a move within a knowing-game. Thus, the skeptic invites Moore's misguided response as well as Wittgenstein's response that he cannot "imagine a reasonable doubt as to the existence of the earth during the last 100 years" (passage 261).

It follows that what Moore and the skeptic are saying cannot be said adequately by talking of knowing and doubting because such claims, as moves within knowing-games, involve appeal to the inappropriate notions of giving grounds and being certain. But Wittgenstein concedes that the skeptic is concerned with a further doubt which must be treated differently, i.e., not by treating it as a practical doubt (passage 19). In response to this view, it begs the question to say that we must "expunge the sen-

6. See also passage 524.

tences that don't get us any further" in knowing-games (passage 33), because the question is whether the skeptic's arguments get us further in some other sense. And it is perfectly clear to Wittgenstein that more must be said.

37. But is it an adequate answer to the scepticism of the idealist, or the assurances of the realist, to say that "There are physical objects" is nonsense? For them after all it is not nonsense. It would, however, be an answer to say: this assertion, or its opposite is a misfiring attempt to express what can't be expressed like that. And that it does misfire can be shown; but that isn't the end of the matter. We need to realize that what presents itself to us as the first expression of a difficulty, or of its solution, may as yet not be correctly expressed at all. Just as one who has a just censure of a picture to make will often at first offer the censure where it does not belong, and an *investigation* is needed in order to find the right point of attack for the critic.

Here we have a clear statement of position (2): what Moore and the skeptic say is said very badly because claims to know and doubt are offered where they do not belong. But what they say disguises what they want to say, which is something worth saying. The problem for philosophy is not to avoid the activity of "censure" (passage 37) but to find "the right point of attack."

SCIENCE AND PHILOSOPHY

One characteristic of the sort of investigation Wittgenstein recommends (passage 37) is that philosophical questions are not to be answered by the techniques of science. Thus, doubting the existence of the world in the last 100 years may be a matter of philosophical doubt not answerable by science (passage 259). To claim, as Moore does, to offer a proof and a refutation is to treat skeptical questions as scientific. Thus, it follows from Moore's practice that philosophical conclusions fail if their proofs fail (passage 408); they can be found true or false by evaluating evidence. A philosophical intention, on this view, is an intention to prove philosophical claims. Wittgenstein emphasizes that he is concerned with distinguishing the use of "I know that that's a . . ." in ordinary discourse and scientific discourse from its use "with philosophical intention." Only in the latter case does he "want to reply, 'You don't *know* anything!'"

(passages 406, 407). His point is that philosophical claims are not supposed to be falsifiable in the way that scientific ones are; in his misguided way this is just the point Moore is trying to make. Wittgenstein's discussion here is critical not because he wishes to ridicule "philosophical intentions" but because he wishes to clarify them, to show what philosophers mean (see 406 and 407) in a way that distinguishes them from scientists.

Let us summarize the argument so far, an argument which is largely negative, a discussion of what philosophy is not. It is not a matter of personal claims to know, supportable by evidence, as scientific claims are supportable; it is therefore not falsifiable and does not involve practical doubt. At the same time the questions and intentions of philosophers are not to be dismissed out of hand. This is confirmed by Wittgenstein when he says that he would be *more willing* to listen to someone who doubted the existence of the earth 150 years ago than to someone who doubted the existence of Napoleon (passage 185). The former is more interesting because he "is impugning the nature of all historical evidence" and "I cannot say of this . . . that it is definitely correct" (passage 188).

A positive characterization may begin with the relevance of the notion of evidence. Assume that a major job (or the characteristic job) of philosophy is the investigation of practices—of thinking, speaking, and acting. Consider the following examples of things that a philosopher may say.

1. The existence of the earth 150 years ago is absolutely certain.
2. The practice of doing history (or alternatively, the possibility of doing history as we are familiar with it) presupposes the conviction that the earth existed 150 years ago.

What does it mean to affirm or deny that either of these propositions is or is not based on evidence, is or is not falsifiable? Proposition (1) might occur in a knowing-game whose object is a historical (geological, etc.) account rather than an account of the practice of doing history (geology, etc.). On the other hand, (2) is unambiguously about a practice. Because (1) is potentially ambiguous, it seems important to ask whether historical evidence and historical research are relevant. Proposition (2) offers no such problem. If (2), unlike (1), is clearly a philosophically relevant conclusion, and if the job of philosophy is the investigation of practices, does this investigation itself involve the marshalling of evidence? The answer is not clear because our notion of evidence is not clear. What matters is that the kind of "evidence" which is relevant to the investigation of practices is largely uncovered through self-interrogation about how one proceeds, about what makes sense, and about what one can reasonably imagine. It is part of the notion of a practice that all persons who share a practice will be likely to perform such self-interrogation in much the same way with generally the same answers. Thus, the investigation of practices is not a knowing-game, an empirical task, in the usual sense; what one "finds out" is, in part, the general nature of finding out.

This leaves many questions unanswered. First, what does it mean to do philosophy badly or well? (The question is complicated for such other practices as doing history or doing science because of the many kinds of mistake.) The distinctive way of testing for philosophical mistakes and refining philosophical accounts is by counterexample. An analysis which says that the practice of history is such that claim x would not make sense is refuted by the example of a context in which claim x is made and *does* make sense as a move in the knowing-game of history. Second, for any hypothetical counterexample, can one decide whether it is or is not an example of a move within the putative knowing-game of history? The answer to this seems to me that one cannot always decide. Suppose we discover a tribe that recounts its past in accord with a notion of cyclical rather than linear time; suppose event x is not spoken of as a single past event but as a circumstance in both the past and the future, recurring in each cycle. Is this a move within history, or is it a practice within a knowing-game that resembles history but is not history? Suppose, as a second example, that we discover, describe, and investigate a past in which the planet Earth did not exist 150 years ago, but in which our ancestors were transported from a different solar system, given "apparent" memories, etc. Does this show that "The earth existed . . ." *is* an investigable historical fact and not constitutive of the practice of doing history?

It seems to me that these questions are not answerable as they stand. First, more needs to be said about each example before we can determine whether it is part of an internally consistent story. Second, the notion of history (of the constituent "rules" of the practice of history) is relatively indeterminate for purposes of these examples. Our stance toward cyclical accounts of the succession of human events as "history" will depend on an assessment of the purposes of such accounts vis-à-vis the ways *we* do history. The notion of history *is*, however, determinate enough for Wittgenstein's purposes, i.e., for distinguishing those matters about which doubt and questioning cannot ordinarily arise from those matters which are the subject matter of historical research. In other words, we can, over a broad range of examples, distinguish characterizations *of* the practice from matters investigated by practitioners.[7]

CONCLUSIONS

I have tried to complement Wittgenstein's tentative account of what philosophy is *not* with a tentative account of what philosophy *is*. A less tentative suggestion is that philosophy is exemplified by what Wittgenstein does in *On Certainty* and by the reconstruction I have offered in chapters one through six.

In the previous section I looked at some unanswered questions about the relation of philosophical questions to questions within nonphilosophical knowing-games like history. There are other unanswered and important questions. We have already seen that it begs the question of the worth or significance of philosophy to say that we must "expunge the sentences that don't get us any further" or to say that claims are significant only if they are moves within *empirical* knowing-games. Investigations of the nature of practices may get us further and be significant in the sense that they make clear to us the nature of our practices, and such self-understanding may be an end in itself. But an unanswered and important question is whether the investigation of the nature of practices gets us further in a second way, whether it has consequences for the practitioner insofar as he is a physicist, historian, anthropologist, and so forth. Does reflection on the nature and use of theories, on the nature of confirmation, etc., itself

7. My argument suggests two points. First, the distinction between a posteriori propositions (or investigable ones) and a priori propositions (or propositions held fast) is inescapable for any conception of knowledge. Second, it is not possible to speak of a priori propositions which, taken together, are constitutive of an enterprise (doing history, for example) because the enterprise, if it is a practice, is not defined in terms of a specifiable set of rules (unlike chess, for example).

change as well as clarify the work done by empirical investigators? It is rash to assume that it does not.

A second unanswered question is whether the practice of philosophy is distinguished by a special vocabulary or special usages of terms. The term "practice" and the terms "empirical" and "logical," as discussed in chapter two, are obvious and uncontroversial (I think) candidates. A sub-question, and one that is important in interpreting Wittgenstein's remarks about philosophy, is whether the term "to know" is part of the vocabulary of philosophy. (This is the same puzzling question as whether investigating practices is engaging in a knowing-game.) On the one hand, as we have seen, "know" is not distinctively or exclusively philosophical; there is danger in confusing philosophy with empirical knowing-games. Wittgenstein says that "know" is correctly used, for example, in the anatomical description, "I know that twelve pairs of nerves lead from the brain" (passage 621). He then asks whether it is not equally correct to use "know" in the propositions Moore offers, as long as these occur "in particular circumstances." And he concludes that "for each one of these sentences I can imagine circumstances that turn it into a move in one of our language-games, and by that it loses everything that is philosophically astonishing" (passage 622). The skeptic, in other words, cannot astonish us by denying that we know, etc., just as Moore cannot take the skeptic by surprise by offering a proof of knowing. But, at the same time, Moore's use is a use that makes sense in particular circumstances, and the circumstances, as in Moore's case, may be philosophical. Even if "know" is not a distinctively philosophical word, it is not forbidden to the philosopher either:

350. "I know that that's a tree" is something a philosopher might say to demonstrate to himself or to someone else that he *knows* something that is not a mathematical or logical truth.... (Here I have already sketched a background, a surrounding, for this remark, that is to say given it a context.)...

Finally, I have not meant to suggest that *On Certainty* is free of ambiguity on these matters, or that Wittgenstein is free of indecision. On the one hand, he offers a dichotomy between (1) empirical knowing-games, which "get us further," and (2) all other claims to know, which are "pointless," "meaningless," and to be "expunged." This view has its roots in the *Tractatus* and can be found in *Philosophical Investigations*. On the other hand, he offers a more satisfactory trichotomy among (1) empirical knowing-games, (2) claims to know in philosophical contexts, in which practices themselves are the objects of investigation, and (3) claims to know that are nonsense insofar as there is no available context. I have tried to show how Wittgenstein himself does the job of investigating practices, how he sketches a general methodology for philosophy by doing so and, finally, how it is that philosophy, as a practice itself, becomes a subject for philosophical scrutiny.

Table of References

to *On Certainty*

When a page number is italicized, the passage is quoted on that page. Otherwise, all references are to citations of passages in the text or in footnotes.

Index

Library of Congress Cataloging in Publication Data

Morawetz, Thomas, 1942–
Wittgenstein and knowledge.

Includes index.
1. Wittgenstein, Ludwig, 1889–1951. Uber
Gewissheit. 2. Certainty. I. Title.
B3376.W563U335   121   78–53178
ISBN 0–87023–250–9